GOLF ESCAPES

A SELECTION OF THE WORLD'S BEST GOLFING HOLIDAYS

GOLF WORLD

MAGAZINE

GOLF ESCAPES

A SELECTION OF THE WORLD'S BEST GOLFING HOLIDAYS

GOLF
WORLD
MAGAZINE

First published in 2003

A catalogue record for this book is available from the British Library

ISBN 1 84425 146 2

Published jointly by
Haynes Publishing, Sparkford,
Yeovil, Somerset BA22 7JJ, England
Phone 01963 440635,
www.haynes.co.uk
And
Emap Active Limited,
Wentworth House, Wentworth Street,
Peterborough PE1 1DS, England
Phone 01733 213700,
www.emap.com

Produced for Haynes Publishing and Emap Active Ltd by
PAGE*One*, 5 Missenden Road, Chesham, Bucks HP5 1JL, England

Printed and bound in England by J.H. Haynes & Co. Ltd, Sparkford

Contents

Foreword

So much to choose from, but is that destination somewhere which offers fantastic golf as well as value? Call in the Golf World experts. In this 160 page special Golf Escapes book that's exactly what we have done with Golf World's well-travelled staff and contributors bringing you the very best selection of golfing destinations to suit all budgets and tastes.

If it's culture you want we have it in spades, if it's advice on where best to go as a golfing society there's tailor-made information, if it's tips on where to eat and drink, then you won't be disappointed either.

Golf World magazine casts an experienced eye over the vast choice of golfing venues around the world and selects for your delictation the places we know you will love going to because we love going there too.

All tastes are catered for – from the foodies who delight in the offerings of Bologna, to the die-hards who want the Myrtle Beach experience, to the traditionalists who want golf and more golf in the heartlands of the Algarve and Costa del Sol.

The range of golf destinations featured is impressive - the Costa Brava, French Riveria, South Africa, Ireland, France, Bavaria, Spain – there is something for everybody.

Now get planning that trip of a lifetime with our help. Good golfing.

DAVID CLARKE
GOLF WORLD PUBLISHING EDITOR-IN-CHIEF

Costa Bravo

The Costa Brava, a 21km stretch of coastline in sunny Spain, has emerged as a popular holiday destination for British golfers. Here we look at what the area has to offer in terms of challenging golf.

Words: **Robin Swithinbank** Photography: **Angus Murray**

A relative newcomer, the PGA Catalunya has jumped to 10th spot in Golf World's Top 100 Continental Europe course rankings.

The North Course at La Cala
has a spectacular backdrop,
making it the perfect place for
a golf holiday.

It's one of the most popular golf holiday destinations with British golfers. Yet it is still possible to get away from the hubbub and play some quality courses on the Costa del Sol.

Spain's southerly suntrap of the Costa del Sol is precisely where you want to be this winter. With a sub-tropical climate and 300 days of sunshine a year, this is a place you can be sure of finding the sun god. From the moment you step off the plane at Malaga airport, you are immersed in warm, languid Spanish air. No wonder then that 20 years ago investors decided to capitalise on the balmy climate and turned the 100 miles of coastline between Malaga and Gibraltar into a mass building site. Hotels, timeshare resorts, restaurants and golf courses sprung up all over the place, turning the area into one of the most popular holiday destinations in Europe. Between 1985 and 1991 no fewer than 17 courses were built, and so the Costa del Sol became the Costa del Golf.

Go, therefore, for the sunshine – but don't go to get away from it all. The Costa del Sol is busy and ongoing construction means the sight of cranes and the sound of hammering are never far away. Don't be surprised either if the majority of the local population – oranged skinned and dripping with jewellery – speak English.

But this is still a golfer's treat. And by looking inland, it's not impossible to find a quieter spot.

Take La Cala, the first destination on my short break to the Costa del Sol, for example. This five-star resort lies five miles from the coastline in the foothills of the Mijas Mountains and boasts two fine courses, the North and the South. The hotel brims with rustic charm. In fact, if it wasn't for the usual trappings of a luxury hotel – high class restaurant, large swimming pool, heated bathroom floors etc – you could be forgiven for thinking it

was the home of a Spanish Don. Indeed, it would have been no surprise to wake in the morning and see vineyards laid out before the hotel, but the South Course is the perfect alternative.

The newer North is lauded as the better course of the two. It's a little longer at 6,769 yards to the South's 6,527, but don't believe the hype. I think the South Course, opened in 1991, is the superior layout.

It fits into the valley far better than its young sibling. The terrain is dominated by the rumblings of hills and hollows, but at no point is this used falsely. Here you are encouraged to think your way round the course, adding a club here and taking one away there to counter the ups and downs of holes that are both beautiful and fair. Bunkers, a couple of lakes and sometimes merciless contours rarely flatter, but it is the South's gorse that will cripple a wayward ball-striker. There's a lot of it on both courses, reminding golfers that it was no mean feat to create such lush fairways and greens in such demanding conditions. The South's par fours are its strong points; the 13th, 14th and 15th being a particularly fine stretch.

The North Course, in contrast, feels as though it has been squeezed into the space available and in places it is rather contrived. A few holes are tarred with the Mickey Mouse brush (with apologies to Disney), the 5th being the most salient example of this. A par four of 354 yards it doglegs right around a valley, three-quarters of the hole becoming a mere spectator.

The other fault with the layout, I think, is that it rarely takes advantage of the setting. The foothills are stunning, and yet it is not until the par three 16th that you really get a feel for them. It's a short hole at only 135 yards, but with views that stretch for miles through the valley it is a jaw-dropping sight.

Overall, La Cala is a superb place to play golf and given its seclusion it has a classier feel than some of the Costa del Sol's coastal courses. The on-site David Leadbetter Academy and a third course, expected to open at the end of the year, add to the attraction.

What with all the development on the coastal strip in the past two decades, it's sometimes hard to see beyond the blocks of apartments to the striking hills that loom magnificently over the area. But venture further inland as I did and you will find wild, natural beauty and ancient walled towns.

Ronda, 50 km inland, is a perfect little town high in the mountains. The drive up is unforgettable along narrow, winding roads that have incredible views back to the coast. But keep looking forward for beyond the wall of hills you will

eventually come to high plateaux and then the town of Ronda itself. Famous for its plunging gorge and the 18th century bridge that crosses it, Ronda is also home to Spain's oldest bullring, which is open to visitors. The quiet back streets are the perfect antidote to bustling Marbella, but it's back to the coast we must head for more golf.

Rio Real is one of the grandpas of the Costa del Sol's golfing community. Built in the dark and distant year of 1965, it has a slightly more mature feel to it than La Cala, but with its close proximity to the effervescent life of the area comes a very contrasting feel. This is city golf, where the sound of lorries and young Spaniards in clapped-out old Séats rings on almost every hole. The old coastal road that links southern Spain's sprawling conurbation traverses this low-lying course and high-rise blocks of flats and villas surround it, but nonetheless this is

very green terrain. Tall palm trees line deliciously carpeted fairways and a river, albeit an almost dry one, runs through the middle of the course – Rio Real, from which the club takes its name. As with so many of the courses on the Costa del Sol, Rio Real is dogged by a couple of crazy holes that detract from an otherwise great layout. Fortunately the remainder of the course is more sensible. It's attractive and relatively challenging, with some long par fours, and will offer a keen opponent to both low and high handicappers. Part of Rio's appeal is that it sits so close to civilisation and yet it is still a relaxing place to play golf.

But I am going to have to save my enthusiasm for a fourth course. The North and South at La Cala and Rio Real all have their charms, but not one sets the senses ablaze quite like Monte Mayor.

Adrenaline junkies talk of extreme sport and will rarely refer to golf as a

"La Cala is a superb place to play golf and given its seclusion it has a classier feel than some of the Costa del Sol's coastal courses"

Rio Real's appeal is that it sits so close to civilisation and yet it is still a relaxing place to play golf.

La Cala South's Course uses the natural contours of the land to provide a tough challenge.

Monte Mayor is a stunning golf course but don't let its beauty fool you. It is one of the toughest challenges in the area.

thrills-and-spills ride, but then they clearly haven't played this, the Costa del Sol's most spectacular golf course. It is such an intense golf experience, set high up in the mountains between San Pedro de Alcántara and Estepona, with extremes not normally associated with the gentle game, that your body will jump with nervous energy from first tee to final green.

It is clear from the outset that this is an exceptionally tight course that will show little mercy to a higher handicapper. This is not a course where your wayward shots will be afforded the luxury of landing behind a green or in a bunker on a parallel hole. Oh no. Here, if you send your ball beyond the initial boundaries of the hole, you will lose it. It's that simple. This is a stage where the performer is gripped both by gut-wrenching terror and the desire to portray beauty. With its gaping ravines, teasing gulleys, chasms in huge

rocks, deep valleys with fresh, cool mountain streams running through them, and wild, non-traversable gulfs of dense flora, it is easy to forget that this is also a golf course. It's just so overwhelmingly beautiful.

At 6,183 yards it's not long, but don't be fooled. The par threes are glorious, not least the 211-yard 3rd, which is stupefyingly beautiful, but hopelessly difficult. If you can't hit a long iron straight you will be taking advantage of one of the hole's two dropping zones. The hole swoops over a cavernous valley down to a raised green that you must hit – if not, recovery is almost impossible. Fun stuff, and although tough enough to bring most golfers to their knees, it is such a gorgeous sight that you'll simply want to hit the best shot of your life, which is what prevents the hole and, as a rule, the course from succumbing to the absurd.

In fact, it is only one step away from absurdity, but it has an inspirational magic that lends it forgiveness. Any sinner will be humbled by its grandeur and only the merciless will overcome its unnerving ability to find every chink in your game.

In every way this is a marvellous experience. Even the clubhouse, which is currently being expanded, has a unique allure to it. If it weren't a haven for golfers wanting to reflect on the course's mightiness, it would be a 16th century monastic community. Intimate, quaint and so easy to fall in love with.

Lap up the sunshine, revel in the golf and remember; whilst at home in Blighty, whether the weather be cold or whether the weather be hot, we have to put up with the weather, whether we like it or not. Tempted to give Costa del Sol golf a try?

The four courses in detail

La Cala North

6,769 yards, par 73.
Built: 1993.
Architect: Cabell B. Robinson.
Address: La Cala de Mijas, Apdo. Correos 106, 29649 - Mijas Costa - Málaga.
Location: 7km east of Marbella, leave coastal road at La Cala de Mijas turning, follow signs to Campo de golf up into the hills.
Tel: (00 34) 952 66 90 33.
Web: www.lacala.com
e-mail: golf@lacala.com
What to expect: Up and down golf in a beautiful setting.

La Cala South

6,527 yards, par 71.
Built: 1991.
Architect: Cabell B. Robinson.
Address: La Cala de Mijas, Apdo. Correos 106, 29649 - Mijas Costa - Málaga.
Location: 7km east of Marbella, leave coastal road at La Cala de Mijas turning, follow signs to Campo de golf up into the hills.
Tel: (00 34) 952 66 90 33.
Web: www.lacala.com
e-mail: golf@lacala.com
What to expect: Fair, natural and consistent golf.

Rio Real

6,745 yards, par 72.
Built: 1965.
Architect: Don Javier Arana.
Address: Urb. Golf Río Real - 29600 Marbella - Málaga.
Location: 3km west of Marbella off coastal road.
Tel: (00 34) 952 76 57 33.
Web: www.rio-real.com
e-mail: rioreal@golf-andalucia.net
What to expect: Established and enjoyable course in urban location.

Monte Mayor

6,183, par 71.
Built: 1989.
Architect: Don José Gancedo.
Address: Arda. Monte Mayor, 29679 - Benahavis - Málaga.
Location: Follow signs from coastal road to Benahavis, turn left up 8km stretch where signposted.
Tel: (00 34) 952 11 30 88.
Web: www.montemayorgolf.com
What to expect: Heart-attacks, for all sorts of reasons, but a great place to die. Seriously, this is the jewel in the Costa del Sol crown. You must visit.

Costa
Bravo,
three ways!

Photography **Bob Atkins**

PGA Catalunya: Your
chance to play a
European Tour venue.

PGA CATALUNYA
Ranked 10th in Golf World's
top European courses.

HOLIDAY 1 If you want...

Simply brilliant golf

What can Costa Brava courses offer that other parts of the Mediterranean can't?
They are not played into the ground, so the maintenance is better. Plus Catalonia is pretty hilly, which gives the courses plenty of character. These tracks are not dull spud field plods. You can't sniff at the Pyrenees as a back-drop either. The European Tour has seen fit to move its qualifying event from southern Spain to Emporda and Pals, a pretty handy endorsement of the quality here.

I won't, then. But I only want a short break. Which three courses must I play?
PGA Catalunya is your priority. The course is a few years old, but is already ranked 10th in Golf World's definitive list of the top 100 European courses. It's good enough to host tour events. PGA offers a series of plunging drives down to immaculate fairways and thrilling approaches over lakes.

Sounds a bit tough.
The course will challenge a tour professional, so the chances are even you will find it a handful.

Well, that's one.
It gets subjective now, but we recommend Emporda and Mas Nou. Emporda is again well ranked in our European top 100, at 59, and its three contrasting nines make you feel you've really played two courses. The first, open with sandy waste areas, prepares you not for the forested and tight other two. But it's a great track with water and lots of tactical doglegs.
Perhaps we should suggest Pals, at 92 the only other course from the Costa Brava in our top 100, as third course, but instead we've gone for Mas Nou simply because it is so different. It may not be a great card-and-pencil course, but its slopes and ravines make this the area's most spectacular course and ideal for holiday matchplay. Plus the

whole course is up on a plateau and offers brain-washing views of the snow-capped Pyrenees to the north and Barcelona to the south. Perfect.

Okay, you've convinced me. What's the best base for all of these courses?
Girona is the logical choice, being as it is near the airport and close to these three courses. But again, the smallness of the Costa means you can stay in a coastal resort without having to drive for hours to get to the courses. But the La Costa resort (00 34 972 667740) at Pals is on the 5th fairway at Pals and very close to Emporda and Serres de Pals.

Are there any courses that just aren't worth it?
Actually, no. Serres de Pals and Torremirona are new and look it in parts, but are still good layouts.

I'm not a very good player. Which are the easier courses?
Torremirona and Costa Brava are reckoned to be a bit more playable, mainly because they offer a bit more room off the tee. Costa Bravan courses are typically very tight.

Any famous designers I should know about?
Pals and Girona owe their layouts to Fred Hawtree, the man responsible for many fine creations including Birkdale and Hillside. Despite the characteristic umbrella pines, these courses still feel British.

When's the best time to play?
During the week. Prices rise by up to a third for weekend rounds, so unless your golf comes as part of a package deal keep it Monday to Friday. But even in the height of summer you can play through the middle of the day without going too red.

EMPORDA
Sample the cultural delights
and then play a round on
Emporda's impressive holes.

If you want...

To soak up the culture

What's the cultural highlight of the Costa Brava?
Catalans love their art, and in parts of the Costa Brava you can't make a backswing without knocking over someone'e easel. King of surrealism Salvador Dali is the region's most famous son. He lived just outside Figueras, where today you will find the Dali triangle – a museum, a gallery and Dali's home. And all within 20km of each other.

Is his work worth seeing?
Well, among Dali's more famous works are Young Virgin Autosodomised by her own Chastity, Apparition of Face and Fruit Dish on a Beach and Hallucinogenic Bullfighter. You get the picture. Dali once defended his general nuttiness by saying: "he only difference between me and a madman is that I am not mad."

My feet start to ache when I look at art. What else is there?
The Bay of Roses is a must. Legend has it Roses gets its name from a unique pinkish light that illuminates the bay. But Roses is definitely the place where the Romans first entered Spain under Scipio in 218BC, and its monasteries and battle sites are a must for history buffs. There is even a section of ruins that appear in the bay at low tide, half in, half out of the water. There are plenty of interesting castles to poke around too. The Castle of Sant Ferran, in Figueras, is one of the largest fortresses in Europe. There is an excellent walled castle at Peralada, near the course, part of which has been turned into a casino. It holds the open air Festival Castell de Peralada every July and August, a showcase for Spanish composers and artists, involving music, theatre and dance. The castle is also a great place for testing some of the vaunted Catalan wines.

What's the Catalan culture like?
The phrase usually used to describe Catalans is 'fiercely independent', and their culture reflects that. You will find plenty of galleries and craft shops chock-full of Catalan art, which tends towards modernist and surrealist themes. They also love their festivals. Lloret de Mar's Dance of Las Almorratxes is held every August 24. It celebrates the time a local woman refused a rich Arab's offerings. Attend the ceremony to find out what he was offering. But the ultimate expression of Catalan culture is a dance, called la Sardana. You dance it in a circle, holding hands with your neighbours while following a confusing sequence of movements. Try it at your peril.

I can do the Hokey Cokey.
I fear that may not qualify you.

What about bullfighting?
If you want to see huge dumb beasts lumbering around a ring and can't wait for the Mike Tyson/Lennox Lewis fight, check out the bullfighting at Girona, Figueras, Lloret de Mar and San Feliu de Guixols on Sundays from June to September.

Where should I base myself for a cultural holiday?
In north Costa Brava. North of La Platja d'Aro, things become a little less touristy. Busy beaches are replaced by pine-clad cliff tops, rocky coastline and secluded coves. And that's where almost all the main cultural attractions are. The five-star Hotel Peralada (00 34 972 538306) offers the only spa in Spain to use wine in its therapy and is right by the course and the castle. Or try the Hotel Aigua Blava (00 34 972 624562), near Begur on the coast – a family-run getaway in the pine trees on the coast.

Where's the best golf in this area?
The Costa Brava is so small that none are out of reach. From Begur it's a short hop to Emporda, Pals and Serres de Pals, and hardly a long one to Mas Nou, Costa Brava and PGA Catalunya. If you're visiting the Dali triangle, check out Torremirona, Peralada and Girona.

> **INSIDER'S TIP:**
> Catalan owes more to French than Spanish, so try to brush up on your French vocab before you go.

19

If you want...

A great society holiday

Which courses in this area do the best society rates?
Check the course guide on page 21. Most courses will be flexible on rates and society packages.

Are there any events which we might base a society trip around?
July 24-28 is a good time to be in Blanes, in south Costa Brava. The local fair, the Festa Major, offers up stacks of activities, the pick of which is a fireworks competition. The prize is the Town of Blanes Trophy. If you fancy entering, buy your fireworks out here – you'll never get them through customs.

What else can my society expect on a visit to the region?
If golf is a little slow-paced for your society, consider coming in Spring.

This is when the annual Rallye Catalunya takes place. The cars follow a spectacular route based around Lloret de Mar. For information, check out www.fia.com

Um, some of the others in the society like a drink or two. What's on tap?
Of course they do. The two big beers are San Miguel and Estrella. Estrella is the local brew and a bit gassier, but Catalans will love you for drinking it. In the hotel bars a bottle will cost you not much more than £1. In the clubs it goes up sharply. Cava, the Spanish version of champagne, is a steal at £6ish a bottle. If you're still thirsty, carajillo – coffee and cognac – is the local popular liqueur. And if you want your socks blown off, try cremat, a

lethal mixture including cognac and rum. The fishermen use it to keep them warm so it must be strong.

What about some food to wash the booze down?
How does chocolate with bacon sound to you? It's not just Catalan art which is surreal; this is the kind of food you can expect to find in the only restaurant in Spain to be given two Michelin stars, which just happens to be based near Roses. Elsewhere expect to find lots of excellent fish dishes, often based on garlic flavouring. Look out for el subquet de peix and sepia. If you see manos de cerdo estofados on the menu, order with caution. You'll get stewed pig's trotters.

Where should we base ourselves?
If you are looking for nightlife, clubs and shops, consider the southern part of the Costa. Lloret de Mar is very touristy and has stacks of hotels. It's also lively at night with bars, clubs and tapas bars to sate most golf societies. Nearby Tossa de Mar is just as good, and both resorts boast good beaches. But perhaps the best society venue is Platja d'Aro, with two fabulous fine-sand beaches and plenty of nightlife including open air cafes, clubs, casinos and night shops. Lively societies could try the Three-star Columbus Hotel (00 34 972 817166), right in the middle of D'Aro's bars and clubs. Alternatively, the Santa Anna hotel (00 34 972 751325) in Estartit is in a fishing village and perfect for quieter societies. It has a good late bar too.

PALS
You'll feel at home on this very British course.

See Barcelona

"Give me a museum and I will fill it." So said Barcelona's most famous son, Pablo Picasso. And the small Picasso Museum in Montcada is one of the unmissables in one of Europe's most cultured cities. Picasso fans will always want to check out his old hangout, the bohemian 'Els Quatre Gats', deep in the winding walkways of the medieval Barrio Gótico, or Gothic Quarter.

Barcelona's 1.5m denizens live in a bizarre mix of gothic, Romanesque and futuristic architecture, thanks to the ubiquitous influence of modernist Antoni Gaudí. One of his more interesting works is the Caso Battlo, designed without straight lines. The city is also benefiting from a recent £1billion facelift and the new marina.

Perhaps the best place to soak in the Catalan atmos is 'Las Ramblas', a mile-long boulevard with markets, cafes, artists, jugglers and puppeteers. Elsewhere, check out the fabulous Nou Camp soccer stadium, the Olympic Village or take the tram to the top of Tibidabo mountain for great views and a spectacular amusement park.

INSIDER'S TIP: Although Barcelona is pretty safe, avoid the southern end of Las Ramblas at night. Pick pockets

MARINA
Where all the rich and famous hang out.

PERALADA HOTEL
There's golf on the doorstep.

The Courses: Where to play and go

Golf Serres de Pals

17256 Pals-Girona
Tel: 0034 972 63 73 75
Fax: 0034 972 66 74 47
e-mail: info@golfserresdepals.com
web: www.golfserresdepals.com

Peralada Golf Club

17491 Peralada
Tel: 0034 972 53 82 87
Fax: 0034 972 53 82 36
e-mail: casaclub@wanadoo.es
web: www.golfperalada.com

Mas Nou

17250 Playa de Aro
Tel: 0034 972 82 69 00
Fax: 0034 972 82 69 06

Club Golf Costa Brava

17246 Santa Cristina d'Aro
Tel: 0034 972 83 71 50
Fax: 0034 972 83 72 72

Emporda Golf Club

17257 Gualta
Tel: 0034 972 76 04 50
Fax: 0034 972 75 71 00
e-mail: info@empordagolfclub.es
web: www.empordagolfclub.es

Club de Golf Girona

17481 Sant Julia de Ramis
Tel: 0034 972 17 16 41
Fax: 0034 972 17 16 82
e-mail: golfgirona@golfgirona.com
web: www.golfgirona.com

PGA Golf de Catalunya

Caldes de Malavella
Tel: 0034 972 47 25 77
Fax: 0034 972 47 04 93
e-mail: agustin.garcia@racc.es

Torremirona Golf Club

17744 Navata
Tel: 0034 972 55 37 37
Fax: 0034 972 55 37 16
e-mail: mironagolf@airtel.net
web: www.torremirona.com

The land of golf

The Algarve has always been a favourite with British golfers, and its reputation for great golf in fabulous conditions and superb weather is as strong as ever. Here you can check out what's on offer.

Words: **Anne Harper**

Sunny, laid back and easy on the eye, Portugal's Algarve has been a perennial favourite with generations of golfers. This 150-mile stretch of Atlantic-washed coastline offers a mild climate all-year-round, boasting an enviable 3,000 hours of sunshine per annum. Access is easy from all parts of Europe, there is a wide choice of good accommodation to suit all pockets, and with 25 courses (plus more on the way) there is a golf layout and green fee to suit every standard of player. Don't ever muddle this Portuguese golf destination with that of the equally popular Costa del Sol. For while Spain's golfing hotspots can be brash and breezy, the Algarve, although busy, retains a more measured, relaxing atmosphere. Its scenery is greener and the environment is not so spoiled by the high-rise development which has blighted much of Spain's Mediterranean coast.

Not that there's any shortage of growth here. Any destination has to constantly seek to reinvent itself to retain its appeal and the Algarve is no exception. Serious money has been poured into Algarvian infrastructure over recent years, beginning with a massive influx of EC funds to create the N125 dual carriageway linking the airport at Faro to

Portugal remains one of the true thoroughbred golf destinations.

the western end of the Algarve and all the small towns and villages in between.

Most of the development is around the golfing enclave of Vilamoura and Quinta da Lago, just a short drive from Faro International Airport. This is where you'll find the ritziest hotels, the expensive boutiques, the stylish yachts moored in the Marina and the lush, top-of-the-range golf courses. Here you'll find Vilamoura Old, San Lorenzo, Vila

Sol and the Royal at Vale do Lobo.

Beyond Vilamoura, the Algarve changes yet again. The low, flat lands around the Ria Formosa are left behind and within 30 miles you'll find an undulating landscape that climbs towards picturesque and quaint hill villages such as Monchique.

Carob, fig, almond and olive trees replace the shady umbrella pines and the Atlantic coastline becomes more

Vale do Lobo...golf at its most spectacular.

ALLSPORT

dramatic, with unspoiled and often uncrowded beaches.

Close to the fishing port of Albufeira you'll discover the linksland course at Salgados, the friendly seaside town of Carvoeiro with its two very different golf

San Lorenzo: Portugal's finest retains its top 10 spot in Golf World's Best Courses rankings.

courses designed by Ronald Fream. Drive even further along the coast and you'll arrive at Henry Cotton's masterpiece at Penina, which has undergone considerable refurbishment in recent years.

Westward still and down a most unpromising side road you will find Palmares, one of the prettiest and

scenically attractive golf courses on The Algarve, and further on is Parque da Floresta, which has the honour of being the last golf course you can play before you fall off of the end of Portugal. Parque da Floresta with its hilly – must take a buggy – fairways claims to be the most westerly golf course in Europe.

ALLSPORT

Your guide to golf on the Algarve

Where to play and how to book. Your golf holiday questions answered.

San Lorenzo is eighth in Golf World's Top 100 list of Best Courses in Continental Europe. I've heard it's difficult to get a tee time there. Is that true?

The best way to get to play San Lorenzo is to stay at Le Meridien Dona Filipa or Penina hotels as they own the course and tee times are restricted to its guests.

San Lorenzo is a beautiful golf course and deserving of the praise lavished upon it. It offers a highly challenging and scenically attractive layout, which runs by sea and the river estuary, through the Ria Formosa nature reserve.

San Lorenzo has hosted numerous professional events and it is not an easy course to play, but offers an enjoyable experience. Handicap limits apply and at the time of writing these were 24 for men and 28 for ladies.

What other courses would you recommend?

Quinta do Lago has hosted seven Portuguese Opens so is an important stop on the European Tour. This is a highly enjoyable parkland layout with spectacular bunkering and lakes, which come into play on a number of holes. Highlight is the par three 15th where you have to carry a lake to reach the island green set in an amphitheatre of umbrella pines.

Vilamoura Old Course is a "must" on any serious golfer's holiday list. Not only does it offer excellent levels of service from bag drop to course marshals, it is also considered to be one of the best in Portugal. The layout undulates through lovely trees and features water on a number of holes.

Donald Steel designed **Vila Sol,** next-door to Vilamoura, and it is considered one of the toughest tests of golf in Portugal, with the first four holes being the most demanding out of the entire 18. Again, it has hosted the Portuguese Open and the course enjoys an undulating and lovely natural setting shaded with numerous umbrella pine trees. It also offers a very classy clubhouse, good practice facilities and tennis next to the clubhouse.

We're very fond of competition golf. Where can we play in tournaments on The Algarve?

The impressive waterside **Marinotel** hosts a week-long golf tournament each February which is now going into its sixth year. The event is attended by amateur golfers from all over Europe and is open to players and non-golfing companions alike.

The tournament is held over Vilamoura's four championship courses, including the highly acclaimed Old Course.

It's a fun week for groups and individuals and starts with a welcome cocktail party culminating in a gala dinner and prizegiving. For more information, email golf@marinotel.pt or log on to www.tivolihotels.com

Bill Goff Travel offers a very good choice of Gala Weeks on The Algarve from October through to May. Their packages include flight, hotel, car hire, golf, welcome cocktail party, gala dinner and prizegiving. For more information telephone 0800 652 1830. Other operators hosting similar weeks are **Lotus Supertravel** on 0207 459 2989 or www.supertravel.co.uk and **Longshot Golf Holidays** on 01730 268621.

Are there any hidden gem golf courses in the area?

Salgados, close to Albufeira is quite unusual in terms of Algarve golf in that it offers an almost links experience, playing right alongside the sea and sand dunes, but stopping a little short to make it a true links course. It's a flat layout with plenty of lakes and offers a decent test of the game in very nice surroundings. The clubhouse enjoys good views, particularly at sunset, and there are some nice restaurants nearby for lunch or dinner.

Pine Cliffs is a really good nine-hole golf course, made even nicer by the fact that it's part of the Sheraton Algarve – one of the best hotels along the coast. This superb little course is always in excellent condition and offers some really tricky holes, particularly the 9th, which runs alongside the cliffs.

Another off-the-beaten-track course is further west along the Algarve at **Palmares**. Many people play it as much for the views as for the course. The first holes start high and drop down to run alongside the sea for five holes. The back nine are totally different, played in a tranquil wooded setting with a stunning backdrop of the Monchique mountains. Great little clubhouse.

Do we need to take our handicap certificates?

Yes, as more and more courses are refusing to let you play without one. If you haven't got an official handicap, a letter of proficiency from your club professional is usually acceptable but it's always best to check with your tour operator.

Vilamoura Old Course... a "must" on any serious golfer's holiday list.

The impressive Vilamoura Old Course will have an equally outstanding neighbour soon...the Victoria.

New course for Vilamoura

One of the Algarve's top destinations, Vilamoura, is to get another course...it's fifth!

Lusotur, the company that manages the golf courses of Vilamoura, is investing 18 million Euros in Victoria Clube de Golfe's new golf course. This is the most ambitious golf project in Portugal, and is aimed at being one of the best golf complexes in the whole of Europe.

The Victoria golf course will be the fifth at Vilamoura and the most exclusive one at the resort, making it ideal to become the Algarve's and Portugal's major venue for top international tournaments.

Famed course architect, Arnold Palmer, whose design company has planned some 500 layouts worldwide, compiled the Victoria course project, and Southern Golf, Europe's largest golf course builder, was awarded the construction contract.

Due to open in April, 2004, the Victoria complex should soon become a prime golf course in Portugal – about 35,000 golfers are estimated to play it yearly, generating revenue of some five million Euros per annum.

Victoria Clube de Golfe's course will be an 18-hole, par-72 championship layout, measuring 6,411 metres from the back tees. Several man-made lakes will provide hazards for the players and also serve as water reservoirs for irrigation.

Amenities include a 1,000 square-metre clubhouse designed by well-known local architect Fernando Galhano, plus a maintenance centre planned by another architect, Paulo Crato.

These amenities, together with the excellent course and first-rate welcoming service to be made available to golfers, will ensure high level personalised treatment for all those frequenting or visiting this spectacular new venue.

The course was specially designed with a view to providing sustainable residential development within the natural surroundings, whilst benefiting from magnificent ocean views from the entire complex.

The course planning guarantees ideal integration into the natural environment of the area, and strict measures are being taken to conserve the existing wetlands and typical indigenous plant life, such as the carob, olive and almond trees.

On completion of the Victoria Clube de Golfe project, Lusotur's plans for golf expansion under the Vilamoura XXI programme will be finalised. This wide-ranging development programme is aimed at making the resort into one of the largest residential and leisure centres in Europe and without any doubt an exceptional golf destination.

The other impressive courses of Vilamoura include the Old Course, Millennium, Laguna and Pinal.

Visiting golfers should take time out to soak in the stunning surroundings of the Lisbon area.

BOB ATKINS

Lively Lisbon

You love playing in Portugal, but fancy a change from the bustling Algarve. Look no further than Lisbon, where golf, gastronomy and culture go hand in glove.

Words: **Anne Harper**

THERE IS FAR MORE TO Portuguese golf than the Algarve. If you've played regularly on that famous strip of Mediterranean coast, you'll know that the courses are fine but the greenfees, and your average waiting times on the tee, seem to increase year by year. For a break from the crowds, and a very different type of stick-and-ball holiday, head north to Lisbon.

The first advantage you'll notice is the climate – not too hot in summer yet relatively mild throughout the winter, ensuring capital golf all year round. Surprisingly perhaps, this is where the game first arrived in Portugal. In the 1800s homesick Brits brought out their

Golf do Estoril's intricate design makes for a challenging and fun round.

gutta percha balls and wooden clubs and established an unusual trading deal – port wine in exchange for golf courses.

Lisbon, like Rome, is built on seven hills, and mixes its rich history and long established culture with 21st century commerce and shopping. It also enjoys a vibrant café society, and you'll find unforgettable nightlife ranging from swish casinos to dramatic fado bars.

There is also a great choice of golf, including designs by some of the best names in the business. It's a mixture of the old – like the distinguished Lisbon Sports Club founded in 1880 – with the new, in the shape of the spectacular Oitavos on the Estoril coastline.

Head just out of the city, and a new motorway crosses the industrial suburbs, bringing the traveller to the old-

established and sophisticated seaside towns of Cascais and Estoril – famous for their stylish restaurants and hotels, along with a choice of superb golf courses including Quinta da Marinha, Penha Longa and Estoril Golf Club.

This area has long been a favourite playground for Lisbon high fliers, and British expatriates too have a long-standing love affair with the region.

Head south of the city, across the yawning mouth of the River Tagus, and you will find yet another kind of Portuguese golfing experience – along the Setubal Peninsular, better known as the Costa Azul.

Some consider this unspoiled stretch of Atlantic-washed coastline to be the 'real' Portugal – the Portugal of soaring mountains and hill fortresses, of historic houses and ancient vineyards. The unspoilt coastline and pristine countryside also provide a superb

environment for animals and plant life, and much of the terrain is deemed to be of international scientific importance.

There is also some simply stunning golf. Enjoy the cunning beachside layout at Aroeira, snaking among soft sand and shady pine trees; or take in the views from the mountainside setting of Quinta do Peru, which wanders through an ancient, once great, country estate. The Costa Azul is also home to the magnificent Troia links course, a Robert Trent Jones Jnr creation, which has hosted more than one Portuguese Open.

However, with the exception of the city itself, don't expect too much hustle and bustle from your Lisbon-based golf holiday. Do, however, expect a holiday with unhurried golf on uncrowded fairways, laid-back nightlife, tasty food, fine wine and a rich history and culture that you'll savour for a very long time after returning home.

MAP: GRAHAM GACHES

BOB ATKINS

How to get there...

...what to see and how to book.
Your golf holiday questions answered.

OUT & ABOUT

■ Lisbon is one of Europe's great cities, and offers all the attractions you'd expect of a cosmopolitan capital. Try a mix of the old and the new with a visit to the Expo '98 development and the Vasco da Gama Bridge. Ancient sites include the Basilica da Estrela, San Jorge Castle and the Monastery of Jeronimos. Modern ones include the Vasco da Gama Shopping Centre.

There is plenty of nightlife to be sampled in the traditional bars of the Bairro Alto and along the trendier Avenida 24 de Julho, while the riverside nightspots offer discos, karaoke and live music. Fado is the traditional Portuguese singing style and soulful renditions can be heard in many bars and clubs hereabouts.

Shopping in Lisbon is superb, with major department stores and a wide range of speciality and boutique shopping for crafts, jewellery, leather, ceramics and designer goods. Most shops are open from 9am until 7pm, closing for two hours at lunch-time. Credit cards are widely accepted.

Eating and drinking is one of the city's great pleasures, and can be done without too much financial pain – there is good food and wine to suit all pockets. Dine out in the High Quarter (Biarro Alto) or Alfama district, where there is a huge selection of decent eateries. Fish and seafood are particularly good, and look out for the region's speciality pork dishes. Try the panoramic restaurant at the top of the Vasco da Gama Tower – but it's essential to book ahead.

Forty minutes south of Lisbon is Cascais, a characterful old fishing village with plenty of bars; and nearby Estoril, with its fine art deco casino – the biggest in Europe. This stands in a magnificent square overlooking the Atlantic Ocean. Despite the age of style being long gone, casino-goers still dress up in all their fine attire for a night out on the town.

Lovers of scenery and history should take a drive into the lovely Sintra hills and visit the National Palace, an old Moorish castle famous for its curious conical chimneys. Even more spectacular is a second palace built in the Parque de Pena, an enormous old estate, and ideal for picnics. Walk or hire a bike to see the grounds.

Birdies & Bolognese

When you play the 12th and
13th holes at Rimini GC you
dice with a watery death.

Delicious cuisine,
breathtaking
architecture, luxury and
finesse. Italy is all this
and much more. Golf
World discovers the
finer side to life and
some fantastic golf too.

taly. The very word resonates with
romance, the height of style in
clothes, classic architecture,
wonderful wines, glamorous
women and amorous men. This is
a country that has thrived on its
reputation for the finer things in life:
from awe-inspiring art to world class
supercars. Even the warmth of its people
and its beaches are in a league of their
own, guaranteed to leave a lasting
impression on every visitor.

But what surprises newcomers to this
country, is that Italy also has some
beautifully kept golf courses. Whilst in
numerical terms it might be miles behind
its European counterparts, for choice of
courses it's leaps ahead in quality and
style: inspiring, challenging and pleasing
to the eye.

Bologna makes a great place to start
your golfing break. Located in the heart
of the Italian boot, this city has its own
airport, and is just two hours flight from
the UK. There are several fine courses
right on the doorstep and you could start
your break at Bologna's very own course –
The Golf Club Bologna.

Built in 1959, it is one of the most
historic courses in Italy. Its classic Cotton
and Harris design is one of the most
memorable in the country. The fairways
sweep up into the hills, with panoramic
views over the splendid sprawling
countryside. From its highest point, some
120 metres above sea level, the fairways
seem to be at one with the surrounding
Emilian hills, rising and falling like the
humps on a camel's back. Golf shots
struck here linger impressively in the sky
above the great expanse of plains that
stretch as far as the eye can see.

At 5,949 metres (around 6,600 yards)
this par 72 isn't the longest you will
encounter, but it is a pleasure to play.
Essentially a mature parkland course, the
added surprise of water comes into play at
the signature hole, the 8th. This 350-yard

You'll be surprised at the high quality courses.

Bologna GC sports 40 years of tree-lined maturity and one of the best clubhouse restaurants in Italy.

par four is a photogenic masterpiece, played over a lake, the hole twisting leftwards to a raised green. It's always a good sign if a course has hosted a prestigious tournament and Bologna can certainly stamp its mark of authenticity on that. It has hosted the Italian Amateur Championships several times in recent years, as well as a number of high level professional competitions. As such, the course layout is constantly being up-dated to challenge the golfer. Recent re-styles include that by Peter Alliss in 2000 who added a new putting green, re-designed the bunkers and completely re-shaped the par four 9th. Alliss chose to fill in four of the bunkers and lengthen the hole slightly in order to bring the steep-sloping fairway approaching the green back into play and reduce the chances of players driving the green.

No visit to the Golf Club Bologna would be complete without taking time to relax and rest your weary golfing legs in the smart and elegant clubhouse. The kitchen is one of the finest among Italian golf clubs. It has been nominated on more than one occasion as one of the top ten restaurants in Italy and is the ideal place to sample the fine cuisine of the region.

If variety is the spice of life, and you're looking for an array of culinary choices, head into one of Bologna's many piazzas. It won't take you long to discover why the city is known as 'The Fat'. Expect to pile on a few pounds with pasta and Parmesan,

fine wine and ice cream; plates full of freshly made tortellini, lasagne and tagliatelle dished up in a stunning variety of shapes and colours, smothered in the best bolognese sauces. Wonderful flatbreads and pastry filled with spinach combine to make a distinct range of calorific delights to please the pallet.

If you can bear to pack your golf clubs away for a few hours, there's no better place to pass some time than Bologna's old walled city, famed for its rusty rooftops and rich hues of terracotta. Named the European City of Culture in

2000, Bologna is home to countless monuments of artistic value. It even has the honour of housing the oldest university in the world, established here over a thousand years ago (in 1088) when 2,000 students from all over Europe poured into the Medieval commune.

Make sure you leave enough time to explore some of the most famous spots. We've all heard of the leaning tower of Pisa, but what about the two ancient tilting spires of the Asinelli and Garisenda? Standing at seven and 10 feet high respectively, they aren't as tall as

The impressive portico leading to...

...the shrine of San Luca in Bologna.

Check out the beach at Rimini.

Bologna's food halls are impressive.

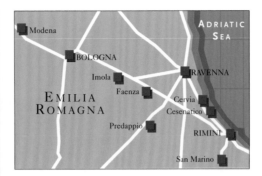

Italy is the testosterone thumping supercar capital of the world and the roots of its famous motor industry are in Bologna.

their famous brother – but equally mind-boggling, albeit clumsy constructions, that leave a lasting impression on the eye. There are 498 steps to the top of the Asinelli minaret; the birds-eye view of the Renaissance townscape below, with its 40km of street arcades and commanding squares, is worth the hike.

Afterwards, if your feet aren't too tired take a wander through some of Bologna's incredible cobbled streets. The porticoes that shelter and shade your passage through this historic city are unique – the longest in the world. When you reach the city centre you'll be greeted by Giambologna's impressive statue of Neptune on the Piazza Maggiore. This is a great resting spot with cafes galore where you can sit back, relax, sip coffee and watch the world go by.

If all this culture is a bit too much for you to handle, and you're looking for some light relief, Bologna has the solution. Italy is the testosterone-thumping supercar capital of the world and the roots of its famous motor industry are in Bologna. Car buffs can visit factories and museums of legendary names such as Ferrari, Maserati and Lamborghini. Factory tours can be arranged, the most popular is the Enze e Dino Ferrari Autodromo at nearby

And the food is of the highest standard.

The Ferrari Museum is worth a visit.

Imola, home of the San Marino Grand Prix.

After a few days in Bologna playing golf and visiting as many of the sights as you can without brain overload, a trip to the coast is the perfect respite. On the way down the A14 you'll pass the fairly new Le Fonti course. Situated in the pretty Torrente Sillaro valley, the particularly mild, healthy micro-climate here provides ideal conditions for golf.

Le Fonti is a newly built course but is already making its mark as a challenging one. A par 72 measuring 6,480 metres (over 7,000 yards) the course is set up for the long hitter. Yet surprisingly it is still a good test of golf without being too intimidating. The course is a lovely spot to spend a morning and lunchtime before continuing your drive south east. The non-golfers in your party will be delighted this is also the Spa capital of Italy with many treatments to refresh and rejuvenate.

The final stop this trip is Italy's main coastal resort – Rimini, home to one of the best golf courses in the region. Rimini Golf Club stretches out across the green Valmarecchia Park, with unrivalled views of San Marino, Verruchio and Torriana. It has an 18-hole championship course with an additional seven-hole executive course reserved for beginners.

The beautiful championship course hosted the 1998 Rimini International Open, one of the most important competitions in the professional European Challenge Tour, and is a fascinating course to play. The softly undulating fairways roll out beneath the stunning Mount Titano and are dotted with bunkers.

Essentially a classic holiday layout, Rimini's fairways are wide to encourage speedy play and suitable for higher handicappers. That's not to say there's a lack of features to entertain the better golfer. There's water and bunkers galore and severe mounding adds to the challenge of a round here.

You're introduced to the troubles from the word go. The first hole is a tough par five that doglegs left around a lake. Your approach is played over water, and if you haven't warmed up your swing and your senses the ball is likely to find an early watery grave. But don't despair if you come away feeling your game has been left in tatters, because there's a first rate teaching academy on site. The driving range is fully irrigated and illuminated and the practice greens can be set up in over 100 different flag positions, 25 of which are covered. So you can enjoy perfecting your game any time, rain or shine.

At the end of the day, there's nothing nicer than soaking up some rays on the sandy white beach that epitomises this resort. There's no need to worry about crowds though. With 15km of the crystal white grains to put your towel on you could mistake this resort for one far more exclusive on a desert isle, pure relaxation heaven. The perfect way to end your holiday is to splash out on a great night in Rimini, a resort bursting with energy and catering for all tastes. From loud brash pubs and clubs, to sophisticated trattorias, you name it – they've got it!

Italy might not be your first choice golf destination, but it does boast some wonderful courses. Plus with so much else to see and do this has to be the ideal destination for a great all-round holiday.

Italian golf
on a budget

For variety, quality, and the family, Italy's Emilia Romagna region represents the golfing place to be this year. So what are you waiting for?

Emilia Romagna is not a tempestuous Italian glamour model. In fact she isn't even female, rather it is a region of northern Italy, and a mighty fine one at that. Home to the Ferrari, Maserati and Lamborghini car dynasties; a wealth of fine food; the occasional drop of red wine; and more golf courses than you can count on the fingers of both hands, Emilia Romagna effortlessly dispels the myth that golf holidays are solely the domain of blokes. This beautiful region just goes to show that

> "Emilia Romagna is not some tempestuous Italian glamour model... it is a region of Italy, and a mighty fine one at that."

there really is such a thing as a 'family' golfing holiday.

The trip starts and ends at Bologna - regional capital, European City of Culture in 2000 and home to the famous pasta sauce. But before licking your lips too moistly there is one thing first-time visitors should definitely know: There is no such thing as spaghetti bolognese in Bologna. Locals refer to the sauce as 'ragu' and anyone who demeans it with the moniker 'bolognese' will be given short shrift and shown the short road out of town. In golfing terms, however, this may not be a bad thing as that very road allows you to turn left in the direction of four courses that offer an eclectic taste of all that's best in Italian golf.

First on the road is the relatively immature Golf Club Matilde di Canossa. Only opened in 1987, the course has yet to fulfil its complete potential, but the undulating nature of the layout allows for many breathtaking views over the wild green landscape of the Matildic lands. Filled with medieval villages and castles, the historic lands span much of the region and host the one tourist trap that should not be avoided: The water-purifying, hilltop village of Saint Pellegrino.

From there, we move on to Parma. Home of the world-famous ham and ideal resting place of one of Emilia Romagna's best parkland courses, La Rocca.

Set in the hills that rise up above the city's suburbs, the course presents golfers with a formidable challenge thanks mostly to the spasmodically-scattered water hazards.

Water also features on the Salsomaggiore Golf and Country Club - a course that takes its name from the city just west of Parma. The club features a wide range of facilities that make golf an experience rather than just a round. Individual and group clinics are available at the complex's Blue Team Golf Academy. And with the beginners kept busy at school, the more ambitious golfer can tackle the championship layout. Famed for its great year-round condition the course meanders through a hilltop valley situated some 360 metres above sea level. And when all is said and done you can meet up in the bar or soothe those aching joints in one of Salsomaggiore's famous spas.

From there, we head North-West to our final destination, the Croara Country Club. Faced with a tight green canvas lacking space due to the proximity of the Apennine hills and the Trebbia River, the designers produced an extremely testing narrow layout that has won great praise from the golfing establishment since opening in 1983. The pinnacle of these plaudits coming when the course was chosen to host the first Italian Women's Open in 1987.

These selections are a mere appetiser of what you can experience at the many courses scattered liberally throughout the Emilia Romagna. Where you go in the region is entirely up to you, but with almost unlimited choice for both golfers and non-golfers, this season's golfing cry may not be "Fore!" but "Forza Italia, Forza Emilia Romagna".

The nearby town that will tempt historians

At-a-glance guide to getting there

■ For more information about golf in Emilio Romagna contact: Emilia Romagna Golf, c/o Romagna Vacanze by Coalce, Galleria Zoffoli 6, 48016 Cervia (Ravenna) Telephone: 0039-0544-973340 Fax: 0039-0544-972911 E-mail: info@emiliaromagnagolf.com or go to the following website: www.emiliaromagnagolf.com

GRAHAM GACHES

Golf Club La Rocca
Par 71, 6,052 metres
Parma
0039-0544-973-340

Salsomaggiore G& CC
Par 72, 5,761 metres
Parma
0039-0524-574-128

Croara Country Club
Par 72, 6,065 metres
Piacenza
0039-0523-977-105

Matilde di Canossa
Par 72, 6,052 metres
Reggio Emilia
0039-0522-371-295

This is not a computer-generated image, this is real, this is Italian golf at its best.

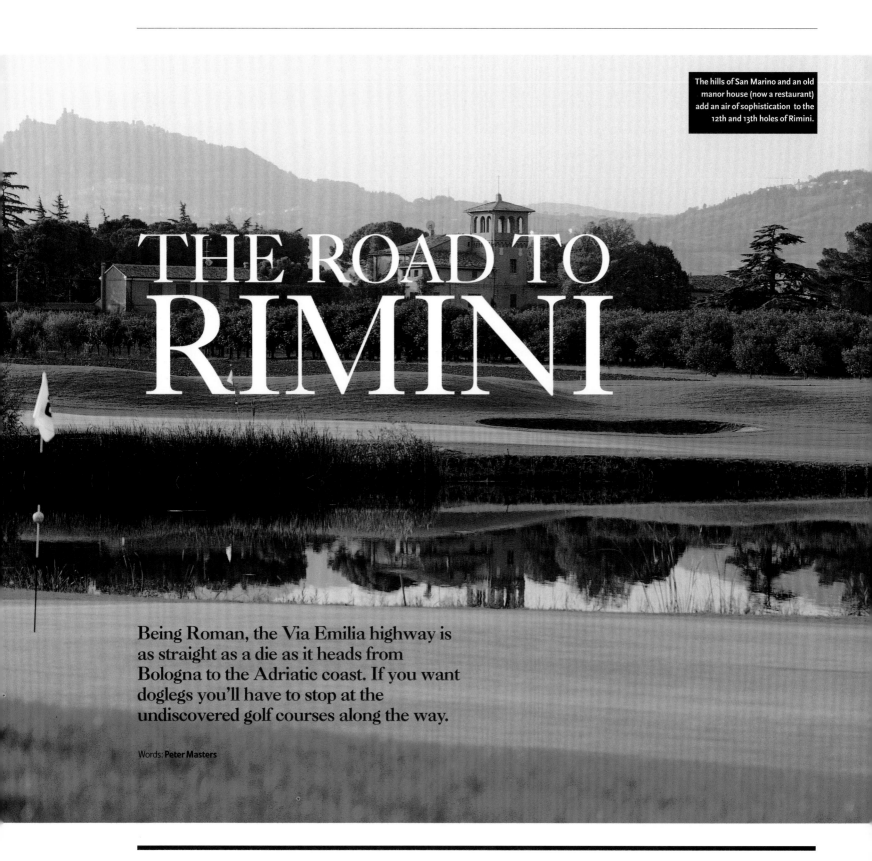

THE ROAD TO RIMINI

Being Roman, the Via Emilia highway is as straight as a die as it heads from Bologna to the Adriatic coast. If you want doglegs you'll have to stop at the undiscovered golf courses along the way.

Words: **Peter Masters**

Maurizio de Vito Piscicelli knows all there is to know about golf in Italy. Ideal, when on a reconnaissance trip to Bologna and he is the man at the airport to pick you up.

"Peter, welcome to Emilia Romagna," he sings with the usual flailing arm accompaniment you associate with Italians. I found myself peering over his shoulder to see if Emilia would help with the baggage, until I realised, somewhat foolishly, that Emilia Romagna was not a person but a region, like Tuscany or Umbria.

My knowledge of golf in Italy had not been top notch. I hadn't known that the country has just 40,000 golfers, 260 courses and that only 120 of those are 18 holes. I hadn't known that along the Adriatic Coast, you could play courses that are virtually empty during the week for as little as £20 a round. I hadn't known either that the dispersal of courses is so top heavy, that at the last count there were little more than a handful in the south.

I hadn't known until Maurizio told me as we headed for Bologna's city centre, that golf has only appeared on prime time television news on two occasions. Once when Costantino Rocca came within a lost play-off of winning the Open Championship at St Andrews and a second time, when the same player scored a hole-in-one in the Ryder Cup at Oak Hill. Both those incidents happened in 1995, so it was a year of golfing overload for the Italian press.

But wait. Rewind a moment. Only five courses in the sunny south of Italy, surely that can't be right?

Maurizio's eyes narrowed slightly and if he'd had a moustache it would have bristled. "It's true," he says, "There are many wonderful places to build courses in the south and it has been tried before. The thing is that when you have built your course you'll find that a man in a black coat will arrive at your door and offer you security. If you turn him down, you will find that your course will be destroyed."

"The Mafia?"

"The Mafia are mainly in Sicily. There are a couple of other groups who control the mainland in the south. There was a tour event at Castelconturbia in 1997 when it was announced that 25 new courses would be constructed in the south as part of a new development project. And how many of those have been completed today? None."

By now we were close to Bologna's centre, where we were to be treated to a guided tour. Such city tours may not be everyone's cup of espresso, but when you are in a city such as this, they are nothing short of fascinating.

Bologna with its Roman history, cobble streets, narrow alleys, mesmerising architecture, quaint cafés in bustling squares and weird pencil thin towers, is not a place you should be in a hurry to leave.

These towers are prevalent in many of the old Italian cities and are a throwback to medieval times when families demonstrated their prowess by the size of their tower. You see in Italy, size really does matter.

In the 12th century Bologna was bigger than Rome itself and the university they have here is the oldest in western Europe. A quarter of the population are students, that's 100,000 of them milling about the streets and occasionally demonstrating, as they were today about trying to stop the war in Afghanistan.

There is a further reminder of an unsettled past at Bologna Station where a terrorist bomb attack 18 years ago led to a number of deaths. The station clock still

"Bologna with its Roman history, mesmerising architecture and quaint

BOLOGNA 5,949M (6,505 YARDS), PAR 72

■ Designed by Henry Cotton and John Harris and situated on hilly parkland terrain about 15 minutes from the city centre, Bologna has a maturity that is quite rare in the region. The course is not particularly tough, but it does have its quirky moments. The 5th, for instance, is an acute dogleg that can be shortened considerably with a drive aimed 50 yards to the right. There are some good holes, especially the 8th, which requires a drive over a lake to a fairway that climbs into the distance.

LE FONTI 6,480M (7,086 YARDS), PAR 72

■ Spread across the floor of the pretty Torrente Sillaro valley, Le Fonti is arguably the best of the new developments. It is just two years old, but plays remarkably well and has enough changes in elevation to make the design both testing and interesting. Look out for the par-4 6th that is played from the top of a hill to a green in the valley below. This is driveable, but there is the added concern of a lake n along the right-hand side. The clubhouse has a wonderful bar and a mouthwatering menu.

ARGENTA 6,300M (6,889 YARDS), PAR 72

■ This was the least impressive of the courses we visited, laid out in rather unimaginative style close to the banks of the river Po, which, at the wrong time of year, can be a haven for mosquitoes. The course is forgiving, in that the rough is plentiful, but not of sufficient height to be heavily penal. As with many of the courses here, you could have the bonus of having it pretty much to yourself. Also on the plus side, the clubhouse has its bar and restaurant upstairs, affording great views of the course.

The Piazza Maggiore is arguably the most beautiful square in Italy.

cafes in bustling squares, is not a place you should be in a hurry to leave"

ADRIATIC 6,246M (6,830 YARDS), PAR 72

■ The first nine holes are an attempt at a Scottish links while the return home is styled around an open plan American layout with water hazards and island greens. The opening stretch falls some way short of the Scottish theme, but it is, nevertheless, a stiff enough challenge. With thick copses of trees and occasional out-of-bounds, you need to favour percentage golf before opening your shoulders after the turn. Former Tour golfer Silvio Grappasonni has been commissioned to build a second course.

RIMINI 6,145M (6,720 YARDS), PAR 72

■ If you can survive the opening hole, which looks to wrestle away your card and deposit it in the bin right from the word go, this turns out to be a good challenge with all the classic modern design features. The opener is a par-5 that curls to the left round a huge lake. A narrow fairway gives little to aim at and if you've not played it before you'll have fun guessing how much of the water you can cut off. With gentle mounding, more lakes and small copses, the rest of the course keeps the interest on a high.

LA TORRE 6,161M (6,737 YARDS), PAR 72

■ Another of the new developments in the Emilia Romagna region, La Torre was opened in 1992 and is only now beginning to show signs of a gathering maturity. This is target golf American-style, with man-made mounds, flat puddle-shaped bunkers and water hazards that are often successful in their attempt at bringing a nervy edge to your swing. For those who are slightly wayward in their approach, the course plays into your hands. It is open enough to offer the chance of recovery for those who can stay dry.

They don't touch, but you'll find that every tower in Bologna is vertically flawed.

Ravenna and its San Vitale temple are sinking quicker than Venice.

reads 10.25, the time that tragedy struck.

The irony is missed that the towers under which the students march were constructed for the sole purpose of getting a height advantage over one's neighbour so that you could zap him with a crossbow when he wasn't looking.

Asinelli and Garisenda can be found at the start of the Roman road to Rimini and they are the most famous of the ancient towers. They do their best to stand side-by-side, but like all the others, they are some way off perpendicular to the ground, the taller one being 97 metres high and leaning by over three metres. The effect of seeing them together is like that impossible art where perspectives are warped beyond reality.

The towers lean because of the sandy soil. Much of Emilia Romagna is reclaimed marshland with as many natural hills and swales as the English fens.

Bologna is set though in an amphitheatre of hills, and atop one of them is a domed cathedral that looks out across the roof tops. Maurizio saw me looking at it.

"That's St Luca. We have a saying over here which we throw down as a bit of a challenge. We say that if you can do that then I'll walk to St Luca with ski boots on."

"And have you?"

"Unfortunately, yes. It's very painful. It's a bit of a dare. Most of the locals have done it."

Also among the hills is Bologna Golf Club which makes it one of the more interesting courses. Maurizio is a fan, but that is probably to do with the fact that his Godfather, I mean Grandfather, founded the club in 1959. Achille Sassoli was quite a character and when he revealed his plans to his friends they all said he was mad to carve a golf course out of the hillside because there was no water for irrigation. Achille, though, was determined and Maurizio tells the story of how he employed the services of a water diviner.

"A strange little man turned up and spent many hours wandering about with his dowsing rods. People found it rather amusing, until he reported back that he had found a large source of water which could be used, so my grandfather had the last laugh."

Henry Cotton and John Harris were the original designers of the layout and Peter Alliss cast his designer's eye over the course in 2001, making a few minor alterations to the bunkers and tees. Of the 27 courses in Emilia Romagna, Bologna is among the best, although you could not put it in the top draw of European venues. This is a pleasant club course – no more, no less.

The draw of this region is connected more to the sophisticated culture of the cities than it is the quality of the golf.

That said, the Italians are catching on now to the potential that golf tourism has to offer.

The authorities there are also looking at some top name designers to create a flagship development which will raise the overall profile. Until then it is cheap golf on very reasonable courses in an area that is literally teaming with character and panache within the many walled cities.

Ravenna and Rimini are on the coast, but my favourite was Ferrara, a wonderfully atmospheric place where the tourist office loans out bicycles for free to anyone wishing to explore the nooks and crannies. The Via Della Volte is a narrow medieval street full of low arches and Via McAllister is named after an Englishman who worked with the craftsmen in Ferrara fashioning ropes that the British Admiralty used for their ships.

If you want to sample the better courses you need to head from Bologna out towards the coast, stopping off at Castel San Pietro to play the new, but quite challenging Le Fonti, before reaching the Adriatic club at Cervia and Rimini.

An eccentric inventor named Paulo Caselli has invested the lion's share of his fortune into the latter and was rewarded by a recent visit of the European Challenge Tour.

A fascinating man, Caselli developed

The fairway on Bologna's 9th slopes heavily from a practice ground on the right which is out-of-bounds.

an irrigation system that is used in a theme park in Brazil, a satellite distance system that doesn't require lasers and a hypodermic needle that is now used in hospitals across America. His gamble with Rimini GC seems to be paying off, although his plans for a major hotel and leisure facility on site still seem a little far off.

The course is used by the residents of San Marino, a country that is best known here for having the audacity to score first in England's 6-1 World Cup qualifier victory some years ago. Seven minutes away by car, San Marino has no VAT and for outsiders it is virtually impossible to buy a house there. For women, the way into this millionaire's retreat is to marry a millionaire who lives there, sadly there is no reciprocal arrangement for a man marrying a San Marino girl. He would be better off grabbing his ski boots and heading off to that cathedral in the hills.

"It is cheap golf on very reasonable courses in an area that is teaming with character and panache"

MONTE CARLO or bust!

The French Riviera is a byword for supreme decadence. But if you're on a budget, don't despair. Steve Carr finds that you can play Monte Carlo without breaking the bank.

Photography: **Bob Atkins**

I pull up outside the glass portico entrance to the glamorous Hotel Hermitage in Monte Carlo, and the doorman shoots a startled look at my small electric blue Peugeot. Very Cary Grant, I like to think. My car contrasts vividly with the two red Ferraris and the silver Lamborghini parked in front of me, but the concierge obviously takes a liking to it, because it is swiftly driven away to a secure parking spot, out of harm's way.

I've already seen how the other half live, and it is rammed home even more when I slink into the world's most famous casino that evening. It's obvious that the high-rollers are locked away in private rooms, because the largest stake roulette table is operating at a minimum bet of 50F (£4.60). Small beer. But it doesn't stop one naïve Japanese lady dotting her red chips around like chickenpox. When she wins she laughs her Gucci socks off, despite getting fewer chips back than she'd laid out. Poor little rich girl – more money than sense.

This is a serious playground for millionaires – and if you glance into an estate agent's window anywhere between Monaco and San Tropez you will see, through green eyes probably, dream houses overlooking the 'Azur'. But as with the rest of the French Riviera, you don't have to be a lottery winner to enjoy Monte Carlo. There is value to be found here, despite the area's reputation for decadence.

Many golfers are put off because they think they'll be stung for everything. Not true. Of course you can sit in pavement cafés and shell out £4 for a beer, but with low-cost airlines, increasing competition between the golf courses, and a list of hotels as long as the Rhone to choose from, bargains are around.

My budget-or-bust golf tour starts at Monte Carlo Golf Club. This is not, as you might expect, in the principality itself (since it's only the size of Hyde Park), but high above it on the slopes of Mont Agel. Founded in 1911, it is one of the oldest

SHADY LADY
The 12th at Royal Mougins is called Parasol Pine, and epitomises the beauty of the Riviera's most expensive course. Below: Monaco harbour is a beauty contest for queen-sized yachts.

clubs in France, and inextricably linked with the Monaco jet-set. I find the atmosphere of the club understated – almost a parody of exclusiveness in that the fittings aren't as swanky as you might expect – but it is very much part of the fabric of the principality's strange sporting heritage, with the Automobile Club at its forefront.

The course itself is not an aristocrat, but rather a down-to-earth gent. At 2,700 feet above the city, the course flatters your long game – a gentle waft floats the ball further than your talent deserves. But although the pros eat it alive – three 60s have been scored in European Tour events here – it is no pushover for the amateur.

Monte Carlo is one of those 'been there, seen it, got the Ralph Lauren T-shirt' kind of courses, and even if your game struggles, you'll be mollified by the incredible outlook from the 5th tee over the miniature city way below. You may of course be unlucky, as I was, since the clouds have a tendency to well up a few hundred feet below you and mask the view.

If you are planning a 'millionaire's' trip, a day or two spent wandering the designer streets – one tiny row of shops includes Dior, Yves St Laurent, Bulgari, Cartier, Piaget and Louis Vuitton – has to be on the agenda too. And an evening drink on your hotel balcony as the sun sets over the harbour brimming with navy-size yachts is a soulful moment.

I leave privilege behind and head for Mougins, near Cannes, a jolly little town in the heart of the Côte d'Azur golfing kingdom. The golf courses here cover the whole spectrum of exclusivity – from mecca to maverick. I check into the terrific Hotel de Mougins, which proudly proclaims that it is only 15 minutes away from nine courses. That might be true if you know the way, but stupidly I don't bother to ask how to get to Royal Mougins – the most expensive golf course on the coast – and set off with just a sketchy map.

MOVING STORY
Tons of earth were shifted to create Royal Mougins, and the 4th hole is a good example of the mounding that guards the greens.

"In the graceful clubhouse at Royal Mougins an elegant lady sashays across the

DOME FROM HOME
Step into the ornate lobby at the Hotel Hermitage, and you'll know that you've well and truly arrived.

For expensive, read private, read exclusive, read no need to advertise, read no signs. I cannot find this holy grail anywhere. Eventually I ring the pro shop and am guided home. It takes an hour and my tee time has gone begging. But the staff aren't worried. I am met, as are all guests, by an elegant lady who sashays across the tiled floor and leads me down to the pro shop and upstairs again to the verandah. Here I take advantage of the three course lunch included in the green fee. A classy touch.

Before stepping out onto the much-

vaunted course, I amble round the graceful clubhouse and admire the oil paintings of Jeffrey Hessing, an American artist who lives in Provence. I want to bottle this place and take it home.

Designer Robert von Hagge had a difficult job with Royal Mougins, because some of the elevation changes in its wooded valley made it tricky to construct a sensible course. He did well, very well – although if you are not a fan of artificial mounding then you might want to look elsewhere. There are some spectacular holes – the 7th is called Roller Coaster

MONEY TO BURN
Monte Carlo comes alive at night, and the casino is the focus for all the fun.

tiled floor to greet me. I'd like to bottle this place and take it home."

and dips impressively; the 12th dives down and right through the pines – but the most exalted of all is the par-3 2nd. There is a drop of around 120 feet from tee to green, and the 'hang time' is more than I've ever experienced when hitting an iron.

I hit one shot that seems to hang onto imaginary rafters for an age before sailing through the back of the green. I decide to have another go and time the descent. Whack. One thousand, two thousand… nine thousand. Count nine seconds to yourself and you will understand what an

extraordinary hole it is. Often these downhillers can be Mickey Mouse, but this one is a belter – I just think it's a shame that it comes so soon in the round.

Having tasted the high life, it is time to discover what else is on offer. The cheapest green fee among the courses I visit is La Grande Bastide, a modern test some 20km inland of Cannes, which works out at £27 for a round. Not bad value, because despite its flat, rather open nature, it is in great nick. The best value I come across, though, is at St Donat, where for just over £30 you can test

yourself against the might of Robert Trent Jones Jnr. Building on an old lavender farm estate, where the ramshackle perfume factory is soon to be converted into a hotel, Jones has made the most of the rocky little river that flows through. Several of the holes are patrolled by the waters, and those that aren't make up for it with troublesome trees and swooping fairways. I find myself impressed by both the course and the set-up.

St Donat also seems to have the slow play issue down to an art. This is a

French connections

Five of the best layouts on the Côte d'Azur, with something for every purse.

Monte Carlo

La Grande Bastide

Grasse

St Donat

NICE

Antibes

CANNES

Monte Carlo MONACO

Royal Mougins

Cannes Mandelieu

St Tropez

THE MEDITERRANEAN

Monte Carlo

5,603 metres (6,127 yards), par 71

Designer: Unknown.

Character: This is a mountain-top course 800 metres above Monaco. Undulating in parts and with a smattering of trees, it is short – and made even shorter by the altitude – but fiddly at times. Very lush because of its position, and often in the clouds, it has charm and a feelgood factor. It will also please some to tread in the footsteps of the world's high rollers, film stars and royalty.

Signature hole: Definitely the par-3 5th, which has one of the best views of any golf hole in the world. The next stop is downtown Monte Carlo, a few thousand feet below!

Call: 0033 4 9241 5070.

popular course because of its quality and price, but rounds do not get tiresome. The club is soon to install clocks on the course that are set to your tee time. If you've been going at the correct pace, whenever you see one you should always be looking at your start time. What's more, rangers have the power to throw slackers off the course – and do, apparently.

I suppose if there's anything to grumble about in this part of the golfing world, it might be the number of people playing. Avoid the weekends if you can, and stick to early morning to get the best run. There's an exception to every rule, however, and at pretty Cannes Mandelieu – the second-oldest course in France – I'd recommend playing on Sunday even though it took me two hours 40 minutes for nine holes. Why? Because the lunchtime buffet is a cracker. It was no surprise to see more low-handicap diners

HOW DID THEY DO THAT?
The village of Tourettes-sur-Loup clings precariously to the hillside above the Riviera, an attractive contrast to the glamour of the coastal strip.

than players making the terrace buzz.

I fly home from Nice (£45 return with easyjet) having decided that even golfing Scrooges can get their money's worth from the south of France. Don't come here expecting to find pay-and-plays by the score, because the emphasis is much more on the well-heeled end of the market – but you must not dismiss the Côte d'Azur outright, because if you are clever you can have a reasonably cheap and very cheerful time.

It is far from a case of Monte Carlo and bust. Come, enjoy the warmth, and live a little – or a lot depending on how fat your wallet might be.

Cannes Mandelieu
5,745 metres (6,282 yards), par 71
Designer: Unknown, but redesigned by Harry Colt.
Character: Set exclusively in a forest of umbrella pines very close to the Mediterranean, the course straddles the La Siagne waterway, which golfers must cross via a small pontoon ferry. Very flat and a little humdrum in parts, but a pleasant setting nonetheless. The par-5s are reachable for the bigger hitters, and scoring could be good as long as you are straight. There's also a quirky start and finish, with par-3s at the 2nd, the 3rd, the 16th and the 17th.
Signature hole: Nothing stands out, but the 6th, a severe dogleg left par-5, is as good a hole as any.
Call: 0033 4 9297 3200.

La Grande Bastide
6,105 metres (6,676 yards), par 72
Designer: Cabel Robinson.
Character: Only ten years old and still maturing, this course is a big, open, modern design with large flat-lipped bunkers and rolling greens. Lots of water too – lakes come into play on eight of the holes. La Bastide is a very fair course and better to play than first impressions might suggest. The clubhouse is comfortable and the terrace overlooking the 18th is a great place to unwind in the summer.
Signature hole: The 404-metre (369-yard) 18th. On the right, a lake guards the elbow of the dogleg, and another pond to the left of the green spells danger.
Call: 0033 4 9377 7008.

Royal Mougins
6,004 metres (6,566 yards), par 71
Designer: Robert von Hagge.
Character: A lush and rolling test through a mixture of pines, lakes and landscaping. No expense has been spared in its construction, and some holes are truly memorable. Proudly exclusive but still very welcoming to visitors, the Royal Mougins clubhouse is one of the finest around.
You'll feel privileged to have been here.
Signature hole: No question it's the 2nd, 'Angel's Dive' –a par-3 that tumbles 100 feet down a small gorge and over a lake. The hole plays more than 200 yards from the back tee, but a 6-iron should get you home.
Call: 0033 4 9292 4969.

St Donat
6,031 metres (6,595 yards), par 71
Designer: Robert Trent Jones Jnr.
Character: Superb value. Great use has been made of a small rocky river that flows through this course, and seven of the holes use the valley very well. St Donat's other holes are on higher ground, and use the wooded estate as their setting. Like most of the courses here, it is busy – deservedly so in this case, because St Donat has a growing reputation as a fine and enjoyable test.
Signature hole: Probably the 3rd, a 177-metre (162-yard) par-3 which needs a good long iron over the snaking riverbed to find the green.
Call: 0033 4 9309 7660.

Where to stay

LUXURY

Hotel Hermitage
Square Beaumarchais, Monte Carlo.
Style: A magnificent belle époque hotel that manages to capture the glamour and elegance of old Monte Carlo, with stunning interiors and an atmosphere of refinement. It has good views out to the famous harbour and is a two-minute walk from the casino.
Best bits: Le Vistamar restaurant has a Michelin star, and produces sublime seafood in a romantic setting next to the Bar-Terrasse once frequented by Princess Grace.
Call: 0037 7 9216 4000; fax 0037 7 9216 3852.

Hotel Hermitage is a monument to the superb architecture of the early 1900s.

VALUE WITH STYLE

Hotel de Mougins
205 Avenue du Golf, Mougins.
Style: A cultivated, unpretentious hotel housed in a beautifully refurbished farmhouse complex. Provençal style with a modern edge, it has a relaxing and friendly feel, and the rooms are understated and homely.
Best bits: Most rooms have their own French windows and a small terrace where you can sip a sundowner, and the pool area is relaxing and peaceful. La Figuière restaurant serves wonderful food and the hotel is only 20 minutes from nine golf courses. The golf package is very good value.
Call: 0033 4 9292 1707; fax 0033 4 9292 1708; e-mail info@hotel-de-mougins.com; or visit www.hotel-de-mougins.com

The cosiness of a farmhouse plus great hospitality – that's Hotel de Mougins.

BUDGET

Hostellerie du Golf
780 Boulevard de la Mer, Mandelieu -La-Napoule.
Style: Very plain and functional, with modern styling inside a neo-Provençal building. No frills, but it does have a pleasant swimming pool and terrace for staving off the heat of summer. Not somewhere you would spend a lot of time, but it makes a good base for exploring the area.
Best bits: A good location near several golf courses and the resort of Cannes. It is also good value.
Call: 0033 4 9349 1166; fax 0033 4 9297 0401.

The Hostellerie du Golf makes a good base, but don't expect too many frills.

Top of the tree

France has more entries in the Top 100 list of courses in Continental Europe than any other country. And it's ideally situated for a short break.

What springs to mind when you think of France? Maybe it's a striking image of the Eiffel Tower, the gothic spires of the Notre Dame or just simply the thought of long strolls around Parisian streets. Those of us with a love of food instantly associate it with the smell of freshly baked baguettes, huge round cheeses, and strong tangy onions. There are so many associations that can be made with France, but golf is rarely at the top of the list.

What you might be surprised to hear is that golf courses can be discovered all over the country. In actual fact, France topped the list of countries with the most golf courses in the Golf World European Top 100 list (November 2001) with 23 entries, three courses in the Top 10 and seven in the Top 20.

Let's face it, as far as golf abroad goes, France is just about as handy as it gets. A short hop across the English Channel on the ferry, an even shorter flight or the simple drive-on-and-off-the-train through the latest convenience – the Euro tunnel.

Most first-time visitors start off in the North of France. This is probably the most convenient option for a weekend break and Dover to Calais is the most popular crossing point. The great thing about taking this trip is that there are several top quality golf courses right on your doorstep when you arrive.

A short drive along the Opal coast, as it is named for its long sandy beaches, and you'll discover Hardelot. Known by locals as "Les Pins" or 'The Pines' this Tom Simpson-designed course is regarded as one of his finest works. In many ways it epitomises the classic British golf course architect, and in true tradition attracts a lot of UK golfers to its fairways.

Essentially a links layout, Hardelot challenges its visitor in all the ways you would expect, blind tee shots, subtle breaks in the greens and well-placed bunkers. The emphasis is on accuracy rather than attacking golf here. Nevertheless, this is the sort of course that once played, will be easier at the second attempt. Hardelot actually boasts two golf courses, but you wouldn't

"If coastal golf isn't your cup of tea, then the more sophisticated fairways of courses around Paris will satisfy your golfing cravings"

believe it, as the other course "Les Dunes" is located on the opposite side of town!

A 20-minute drive further down the coast will bring you to the upmarket seaside town of Le Touquet. This has long been a favourite haunt of France's elite, its stylish shopping galleries and smart, expensive shops catering for a niche market. There are also three great golf courses here, the most well-known is the Harry Colt-designed 'La Mer.' It's easy to see how this course got its name as it boasts wonderful views out over the English Channel. You are forgiven for being distracted by the scenery as the course is mainly sculpted around the rugged and wind-swept dunes of the coast, offering visiting golfers a magnificent landscape.

At 6,330 metres (that's nearly 7,000 yards) this par 72, is certainly not a course for the faint-hearted. There are many features that make it worthy of its ranking (84th) in the 2001 Golf World European Top 100 list, but the views have to be high up there. The course is moderately hilly,

with carefully designed fairways, a few formidable bunkers and some greens that are hidden among the sparse vegetation that often comes into play. The dunes are perhaps the most spectacular feature, and add to the intrigue of each hole. As with all true links golf courses, this one is at its most challenging when the wind blows, making it a tough course for higher handicappers but a good challenge for the seasoned golfer. Little surprise then, that it has played host to the French Open and several French Amateur Championships over the years.

BELLE OF THE BALL

The final course on this coastal trek is Belle Dune. Its beauty, as the name suggests, lies in amongst the natural sand dunes that flank the coastline in this region. The funny thing is, much of the course actually nestles in woodland environs, but it is always the links holes that linger most in the memory. Most visitors would agree that this par 72 is a links course with some of the most amazing holes you will ever see. Huge

COURSES FACTFILE

Le Touquet (La Mer), 6,330 metres, par 72.
Address: Avenue du Golf F-62520 LE TOUQUET. **Tel:** 0033 321062800.
Location: Just off the A16 from Calais. Exit 26, cross bridge, turn left at third traffic light.

Belle Dune, 5,513 metres, par 72.
Address: Promenade du Marquenterre, F-80790 FORT-MAHON-PLAGE.
Tel: 0033 322234550.
Location: 25km to Touquet.
Playing restrictions: The course is closed every Friday from Mid-November to Mid-February.

Hardelot (Les Pins), 5,870 metres, par 72.
Address: 3 Avenue du Golf F-62152 HARDELOT. **Tel:** 0033 321837310.
Location: 15km south of Boulogne.
Playing restrictions: None – the course never shuts.

Chantilly (Vineuil), 6,396 yards, par 73.
Address: Golf de Chantilly, F-60500 CHANTILLY. **Tel:** 0033 344570443.
Location: 41km North of Paris, 2km from Chantilly.
Playing restrictions: Play only on Monday, Tuesday, Wednesday and Friday.
Trolley hire: No buggies available.

Le Golf National (L'Albatros), 6,515 metres, par 72.
Address: 2 Avenue du Golf, F-78280 GUYANCOURT. **Tel:** 0033 130433600.
Location: 14km south-east of Versailles, 30km south of Paris.
Playing restrictions: No restrictions.

Les Bordes, 6,412 metres, par 72.
Address: Golf International des Bordes, F-41220 SAINT-LAURENT-NOUAN.
Tel: 0033 254877213.
Location: 30 km from Orleans.
Playing restrictions: No restrictions.

imposing sand dunes, pretty pines, and a distinct feeling of wilderness, capture the experience. In addition, several of the greens are blind and some have slopes that are a bit ridiculous, even for the thrill-seeking player, but that is more down to the natural contours of the land than the architect's eye. The hills on this course mean a buggy is a must for the less fit among you. The great thing about Belle Dune is that it is a public course, and has no restricted access, and the green fee, priced at 28 Euros on weekdays, is a bargain.

If coastal golf isn't your cup of tea, then perhaps the more sophisticated fairways of courses around Paris will satisfy your golfing cravings. The capital of France, is in many ways, also the golfing capital of the country. Courses certainly aren't in short supply, and they tend to cater for the upper-class market who want to play the best courses in the land. There are more sophisticated and exquisite golf courses around Paris than anywhere else in Continental Europe. Consequently green fees aren't cheap, but what you will get is an immaculately presented golf experience.

Chantilly is one of these courses. Just 25 minutes on the train from the main station (Gare du Nord) make this an appealing choice for most visitors. A Tom Simpson design, the Vineuil course at Chantilly is highly regarded as one of France's finest examples. Not surprising then its ranking as 4th best course in Europe in the Golf World poll. Established in 1909, this is essentially a flat course, set in peaceful forest surroundings. Yet at over 7,000 yards off the championship tees, this golf course is certainly challenging. The best players will think their way around the golf course – strategy will defeat technical ability.

HOME OF FRENCH FEDERATION
If you are looking to play a slightly more accessible course then Le Golf National, home of the French Golf Federation, is the place to head. The "Albatross" is a purpose-built tournament venue that can be discovered in the south-west corner of

Paris. As such the course has been crafted with spectators in mind. It has a mixture of US-styling and links holes set amongst artificial dunes. Each hole is defined by a number of hazards, making them unique and challenging. Whoever decided to put a golf course here certainly had a spark of imagination, as the course was basically created by dumping millions of tons of waste onto the land, and shaping this very effectively into grassy dunes. It is big, challenging and fun, and completely unexpected when you visit for the first time.

Paris is a wonderful vibrant city, with bustling brasseries and elegant hotels. There's plenty to distract the eye with an array of world famous architecture to admire. But if you are a player in search of

a true 'Golf Escape' then you simply have to make the extra journey down to the Loire Valley. Just one-and-a-half hours drive south of Paris you will discover Les Bordes, ranked 7th in the Golf World European Top 100. Set in the heart of the Sologne Forest this former private hunting ground of the entrepreneur Baron Bich (of BiC pens) is truly that – a millionaire's playground.

No expense has been spared in the construction of this championship course. It's not only pleasing to the eye, but challenging to your game. Les Bordes' strength is in its variety of layout. It makes the most of the natural surroundings of forest and water. Every hole is unique.

The real charm of a visit here is the

The highly-rated Les Bordes offers plenty of variety.

tranquility and character of the estate. Every effort has been made to keep it traditional in style. Accommodation is in converted farm buildings, and dinner is served up in front of a huge open fireplace. This is the sort of course you make the effort to book a weekend break at if you are really looking to spoil yourself – it is well worth the extra couple of hours drive to discover it. It truly is a hidden gem.

France literally has a veritable selection of courses in every part of the country. Just take a look at what's on offer further south.

France is the perfect place to combine a family holiday with a few rounds of golf. As well as enjoying the sport on offer there's plenty for visitors to see and do.

Travel south for top sport

Travel a bit further south and sample the delights of Biarritz and Bordeaux. Basque and French influences mingle to create a feeling of well-being and joie de vivre. From the rocky cliffs that Biarritz sits atop, the shoreline stretches north and is one long, wide sandy beach backed by pine forests all the way to Gironde estuary north of Bordeaux through which three of the region's stars run. Moliets is about an hour away from Biarritz, and is a mix of not desperately tight seaside and forest holes.

Seignosse is rated highly, and is manufactured golf, with Robert Von Hagge's trademark hummocks and water hazards ruling the roost. It is at times both dangerous and yet strangely fun. The greens have to be seen to be believed with their on-the-edge borrows.

Hossegor nearby is the oldest and most traditional. Flat and an easy walk with tees and greens close together, and what you see is what you get holes. It is shady and subtle to Seignosse's surreal assault.

Just on the outskirts of town can be found the antidote to the forest golf further north. Chiberta is Tom Simpson's links legacy to southern France, and it rumbles along relatively flat and sandy ground above the surf. With a smattering of trees and strategic bunkering, she is a pleasure in any weather.

So too is Golf du Medoc, just north of Bordeaux some two and a bit hours away. It is best described as an inland links, with a gorse-studded landscape and sandy soil. It is a stone's throw from the great wine chateaux of the world and the added benefits that brings. They do know how to live down here – and eat too – and the outdoor life is close to their hearts. Great sport in great surroundings.

> "The greens at Seignosse have to be seen to be believed with their on-the-edge borrows"

The Secret Playground

Deep in the Loire Valley lies a golf course built on ink. Les Bordes was the private paradise of Baron Bich, the Bic Biro tycoon. Today, you can play it too. Steve Carr visits this and four other courses which began life as the playgrounds of millionaires.

BICH AND FAMOUS
Marcel Bich left more than
ballpoint pens as his legacy.
This is the 8th hole at Les Bordes.

Somebody once described the Bic biro as Socialism in action. Passed from hand to hand in just about every office worldwide, the humble disposable pen belongs to no one, is useful to everyone, and serves the common good. So a visit to Les Bordes, in the Loire Valley, is quite an eye-opener. This is the ultimate in sporting decadence, a golf estate founded on immense wealth and designed to caress the most refined tastes. Yet this is the house that Bic built.

After playing the course, all I can say is thank goodness for old-fashioned capitalist affluence. Without it, we golfing hoi polloi would be robbed of some of the world's finest courses. Because when an exceedingly wealthy man gets bored of making his millions, he often likes to spend it on some frivolous, 'money no object' scheme – and often on a luxuriant piece of real estate with startlingly expensive fairways wriggling through the woods.

Baron Marcel Bich was just such a man. As a humble ink technician in 1940s Paris, Bich saw the potential of an ingenious design by a Hungarian called Laslo Biro, and proceeded to become a millionaire. Within just three years of acquiring the rights to Biro's brainwave, the Societe Bic company was selling 42 million pens a year. Add four million cigarette lighters and nine million razors,

and you have a business based on staggering numbers. Disposable income from disposable commodities. The original Rich Bich, perhaps.

Les Bordes is Baron Bich's exquisite legacy to golf, a remote treasure in the Sologne region 30 miles south of Orleans – where another French icon was burned at the stake. Golf came to the sporting baron late in life, in 1982. His aristocratic ways were more attuned to Roland Garros and Les Sables d'Olonne than St

Andrews. But when a heart attack forced him off the tennis court and the ocean waves – he'd led four Americas Cup jaunts in the '70s – his Japanese business partner Yoshiaki Sakurai enticed him onto the golf course. At 68, like so many before him, Bich was hooked. From then on he devoted his down-time to the links.

Les Bordes – or Chez Bich as it is known in France – sprung from his new-

Memorial to a friendship.

"Baron Bich was delighted with the course – a brave amalgam

How's this for attention to detail? The doorhandles at Les Bordes are made from putter heads. It's called getting you into the mood.

found fervour for the game, and he had a willing accomplice in golf nut Sakurai, whom he trusted implicitly. Together they hatched a plan – to build a no-expense-spared course for their own delectation. They chose Bich's hunting estate in the Loire Valley, where the only sounds to be heard were the twittering of birds, the hooves of wild boar gallivanting through the forests, and the odd crack of a 12 bore.

With the help of American architect Robert Von Hagge, the site was transformed, and today you will also hear the ring of titanium around the ancient oaks and the chattering of contented golfers lounging on the clubhouse verandah. But can money buy you love?

Bich and Sakurai were delighted with the course – a brave amalgam of styles that somehow work together. Apparently Bich objected to only one hole – the par-3 16th. It is an uphill long iron to a plateau green with ludicrous drop-offs into the woods, especially to the left. Von Hagge was also unsure about it, and as he piled up the earth to create this monster, he kept asking his perfectionist client for his views.

CORPORATE GOLFERS

More rich men who treated themselves to a golf course.

John D Rockefeller

Overhills Golf Club,
North Carolina

■ Once the richest man in the world, Rockefeller enlisted the legendary architect Donald Ross to design a private nine holes on his Overhills estate. It was exclusively for Rockefeller and his friends to use. The course is now defunct after being taken over by the US Army, but plans are afoot to rediscover the lost gem.

Steve Wynn

Shadow Creek, Las Vegas

■ This casino and hotel impresario, the man behind some of Vegas' biggest names, has created an oasis out of the flat desert scrub. At first only those high rollers gambling $100,000 in one of Wynn's casinos could get a chance of a game. Today it is open to anyone staying at an MGM Mirage property in Vegas.
Contact 001 702 791 7161.

National Cash Register

NCR Country Club,
Kettering, Ohio

■ Not a single man's dream this time, but one firm's way of giving its employees a fantastic place to spend their leisure time. Not a bad company perk. The NCR workers have such a fine facility that it ranks in the top 100 golf courses in the US and has staged the USPGA, won by Ray Floyd in 1969, and the 1986 US Women's Open.

Michael Smurfit

K Club, Dublin

■ Smurfit is chairman of the Smurfit Group, one of Europe's biggest packaging businesses, and bought the Straffan House estate in 1988. It will stage the 2005 Ryder Cup as well the annual Smurfit European Open. One of the most sought-after rounds of golf in these islands.

# of styles that somehow work together."

No words were forthcoming until finally it was complete. Von Hagge asked for the last time.

"It's nonsense!" came the succinct reply.

Most would agree with Bich – the 16th is definitely the weakest link in an otherwise tranquil and exacting chain. Every other hole at Les Bordes is memorable – some for their wild, natural look with fairways bordered by forest, wildflowers and grasses; others for their man-made muscularity, with railroad-tied greens jutting out into lakes teeming with carp.

The airy lounge bar.

Everything about Les Bordes oozes quality,
including the well designed clubhouse.

The first hole at Les
Bordes makes the start to
your round very tough.

Not one hole follows the direction of its predecessor, and the layout is packed with subtleties and demands bravado in spades. In fact, it is as tough and uncompromising as its original owner. The course record is just 71 (one under par) by Jean Van de Velde, who used to be attached to the place, and who once came under fire from Bich for refusing to practise in the rain.

You can be beaten by its power – and by its hazards if they invade your psyche – but the course is mostly fair. What's wrong with an island green, especially at the end of a par-5? Nothing if it is accommodating and you are good enough! But the wet stuff that appears on 12 of the holes will be intimidating to lesser souls. However, even those who tremble at the sight of a water fountain and go through a dozen balls a round will still find this place a delight. Indeed, it is difficult to tear yourself away from golf even after you have taken on the beast of an 18th, because the practice ground is wonderful and the putting green is one of the finest you'll ever see.

Running down from the rustic yet refined clubhouse to a lake, the gigantic green is a doughnut shape with a bench and an antique statue of a wild boar at its heart. A sculpture by Rodin looks on as you tackle the contours. With a bottle of Chinon at the side, many happy hours can be spent deep into dusk – and beyond in my case.

But what is really special about the course – and something its creators were keen to preserve – is the vast, secluded feel of the estate it runs through. Wildlife still roams freely; deer dart from behind trees; and at the end of the day, you will see birds of prey circling overhead and families of coypu (large water voles) nuzzling around the greens looking for something tasty to eat.

And if you are out early enough to see the steam eddying off the lakes as the dawn sun flickers into life, you will also see a team of devoted greenstaff lovingly tending Les Bordes' immaculate fairways. I watched a man cut by hand the vast 1st green in its island of sand, and calculated that he would walk well over a kilometre before it was done. This attention to detail has made Les Bordes famous – although it remains an isolated and undervalued place.

Men of means often seek havens like this, where they can displace worries about PE ratios and the falling value of the Euro with worries about three-putting the rolling greens. But today, Bich's estate is open for all to find solace, and despite his death in 1994 his classy legacy lives on.

An original Rodin sculpture watches over the practice green at Les Bordes – its head-in-hands attitude ideal for the setting!

The 18th at Les Bordes makes the perfect climax to a course with a sensational setting.

PLANNING YOUR TRIP

Getting there
■ Golf International Les Bordes is 90 minutes south-west of Paris and 30km from Orleans, near the Loire river town of Beaugency, just off the A10 peage. Nearest airports are Paris Orly and Poitiers. Ryan Air www.ryanair.com; 0871 2460000)

The course
■ Les Bordes was ranked 14th when *Golf World* last ranked the Continent's top 100 courses in November 1999. From the white tees, it measures 6,409 metres (7,011 yards); from the yellows 6,023 metres (6,589 yards).

Staying at Les Bordes
■ Baroness Bich was put in charge of the clubhouse, and the golf chalets that overlook the 18th hole.
The 40 rooms and the bar and restaurant are restrained and homely.
　The restaurant serves wholesome, imaginative food with local produce to the fore. And the winelist contains the Baron's own label Grand Cru St Emilion and Chateau de Ferrand, although the fruit-laden Chinon is better value.

Off the course
■ The Loire Valley is famed for its wondrous chateaux. Within easy driving distance you can visit the 'three Cs' at Cheverny (where there is also a golf course), Chambord and Chaumont. Within an hour or so there are the wine villages of Vouvray, Bourgueil, Chinon and Saumur, as well as the ancient cities of Tours and Orleans with their majestic cathedrals.

More details
■ Call 00 33 254 877213; fax 00 33 254 877861; or visit www.lesbordes.com

The 1st hole is set among a wilderness of humps and hollows.

The par three 16th hole is one
of the hardest on the course.

Haus music

Famous for its leather shorts, fruity beers and oompah bands, Bavaria is also an emerging golf destination. Peter Masters swings to the sound of cow bells.

Photography: **Angus Murray**

t's true, in Bavaria the hills really do come alive with the sound of music. It's not a load of Von Trapp, honest. Just pull over in your car, wind down the window and listen.

Bells.

Not church bells, but cow bells. The gentle jingle-jangle, the volume rising and falling on the wind, makes a beguiling countryside anthem. The world's largest percussion orchestra striking a chord for nature as it noshes grass.

Welcome to southern Germany, land of the musical cows.

There really is no mistaking Bavaria – provided, of course, you're not comparing it with its immediate Alpine neighbours. For a start it is incredibly green. Greener than England green. There is none of the magnolia beige of

wheat and barley fields: there are no fields, just a rich, luscious carpet of grass.

Then there is the architecture. Wonderful country houses peep at you from their lofty hillside perches, each framed by cylindrical towers with large blobs of icing on top shaped like giant onions. You know you're in Bavaria when every townhouse wears a geranium necklace and every village is cloaked in the yeasty, hoppy smell of its local brewery (of which there are literally hundreds). You know you're in Bavaria when, in October, grown men can wear tight leather shorts and a cap with a feather in it, and get away with it.

You can get away with quite a lot in Bavaria and I think I know who started it. King Ludwig II died almost 115 years ago, but his spirit lives on across the land, in the fairytale castles that he built and the bizarre life that he led.

ONLY IN BAVARIA...
This is the halfway hut at Mangfalltal.
Rumours of an oompah jukebox are,
sadly, unfounded.

The beflowered clubhouse at Tegernseer hardly
prepares you for the adrenalin rush of some of
the course's holes – especially the 14th (far left).

If you like beer, you'll love Bavaria; this is just
one of thousands of varieties on offer, and it
slipped down a treat.

You can't be in Bavaria that long before someone somewhere recounts a good Ludwig anecdote. His life was an extraordinary composite of political intrigue, muddled sexuality and acts of rampant insanity.

When he came to the throne at the age of 18, in 1864, Ludwig quickly realised that he didn't much fancy his duties as a political leader. He was forced to spend a minimum of 21 days a year in Munich, during which he adopted the curious habit of taking nocturnal rides to various outlying village destinations. He'd ride round and round until he felt he had gone far enough, and then dismount and have a picnic lunch. It was never proven whether Ludwig was actually insane or

not, because for all the odd things he did, he also had ideas of great clarity. He was an obsessive fan of Wagner, and the Opera House on the banks of Lake Forggen is testimony to that. He was eager as well to see the building of the first flying machine – crazy then, but not so crazy now.

But what chance did poor Ludwig have? He came from a family with the ga-ga gene specially inbred in it. His brother Otto was completely barmy, and his aunt suffered from the mistaken impression that she had accidentally swallowed a grand piano made of glass.

Ludwig's enemies appear finally to have caught up with him, because he was pronounced insane in 1886 and died the

Mangfalltal's 17th. Blind shots abound on this back nine.

Even the shops have turrets, spires and towers here. This is Bad Aibling.

next day. His body was washed up on the shores of Lake Starnberg with that of the doctor who had signed the certificate. Murder? Suicide? Accident? No one knows.

His effigy, though, is all over the place, and my first introduction to him comes when I see his face on the dimples of my opponent's golf ball. Dieter Jung runs the Romantik Linder Hotel in Bad Aibling, a busy spa town to the south-east of Munich, and it is he who tells me of Ludwig's exploits as we explore the delights of Maxlrain golf course on the outskirts of the town.

Delights is not overstating it either. Golf has really taken off in this region of Germany, and any number of new courses have sprung up in the last ten years. The standard of many of these, it has to be said, is not that high. For the most part we are not talking championship tests like you might find in the Algarve. The Germans are quite new to the game and many would not cope with those grades of difficulty.

Maxlrain, however, is the exception that proves the rule. It is owned by Prince Erich von Lobkowicz, who lives in the castle and runs the brewery that is also on site. A big man with a big handshake, which I discover to my cost, he has a finger in umpteen business pies and a shrewd financial brain.

For example, the prince didn't want to spend a bucket load of marks on a Langer or a Faldo when he felt a lesser named designer could do just as well. In Peter Krings, a top German amateur, he chose wisely, and Maxlrain has a reputation as

> "Dr Franz Berktold-Fackler looks like a man accustomed to be taken seriously... but his leather shorts and white bony legs make it hard to create a sensible first impression."

It's all down to the size of your window boxes.

one of the best courses on Bavaria's golfing CV.

But back to my partner, Dieter Jung. He is a veritable mine of information – perfect for a travelling hack who knows little more about Germany than what he's seen on Fawlty Towers.

"You know Hitler was here, right in my hotel," he says, as I line up a tricky six footer for a half.

"He didn't have my room, did he?"

"I don't know, but we have pictures taken of him when he arrived."

I hadn't mentioned the war, he had, and he wasn't going to get away with it.

"So did Adolf spend much time in this area during the war?" I ask.

"He started his party in Munich," says Dieter – and then, pointing over some trees, he adds: "About a kilometre over there, the allies imprisoned a quarter of a

Peter's boggy lie

You won't find Liz Hurley and chums advertising this anti-wrinkle treatment.

It's got to be a con. Twenty minutes in a bathtub of hot dirt which, even after 20 minutes of rinsing with a spray jet, still clings to certain body parts – and then you have to pay for the privilege. Bad Aibling is renowned for its peat baths, which are supposed to refresh the parts in a way that Radox can only dream of.

I do my very best to enjoy it and I suppose as a one-off experience, it is well worth it, but I'm not sure I'd do it again. You climb in totally starkers and as the black gunge edges its way into all your nooks and crannies, you are supposed to relax, lie back and think of... well, England.

As your mind wanders, you start feeling about in the murk, finding little bits of twig which disintegrate between your fingers. I'm sure there are those who would absolutely love the experience – hippos for a start – but I am quite relieved to get out and mildly dismayed to find the earthy smell that emanated from the pool stays with me for the rest of the day.

Of course, the whole thing is supposed to be very good for you. Many famous people have immersed themselves in peat, including various famous composers such as Berlioz. Ironic really – composers in a pile of decomposing mulch...

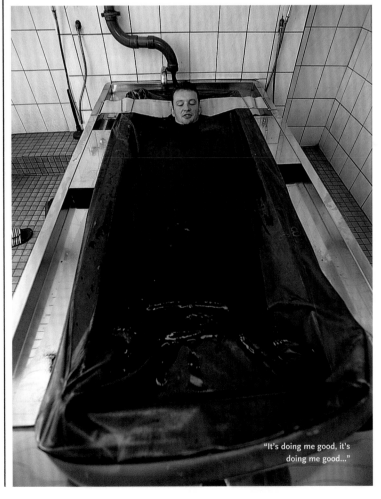

They do this all the time in Bavaria, apparently.

"It's doing me good, it's doing me good..."

The 8th at Maxlrain: By now you'll be ready for a sit-down.

million German troops when they began their push on Berlin."

The conversation changes as we come in sight of the brewery. "They produce 25,000 litres a day and have five different types of beer, from light pils to dunkel, which is dark," Dieter explains.

The Oktoberfest is a huge part of the Bavarian calendar. Eight million visitors descend on Munich in the space of a fortnight, all the hotels are full and everyone ends up tripping over imaginary kerbs and denting their tankards.

Over dinner at the hotel, which dates back to the year 600, we sample each of those beers and talk more about the coming festivities.

"Then there's the festival of cheeses at Oberammergau, where they bring actors in and everybody dresses up as cheeses," smiles Dieter.

"They dress up as cheese? You mean you wander about looking like a piece of Gorgonzola?" I say, struggling with the concept.

Jung looks equally perplexed. "No, I said Jesus, not cheeses. They do it every ten years and stage moments from the Bible. They select who is going to be the Messiah, and that person doesn't cut his

hair for three years."

It sounds like another of Ludwig's ideas, but we don't go into that.

The trip south and west takes us up into the Alpine foothills to Lake Tegernseer. The town of Bad Wiessee borders the lake and is home to one of the oldest clubs in the region. From November to April the landscape is covered in a snowy white blanket, but in the summer this melts away to reveal Tegernseer, a layout that would be an absolute gem but for the presence of two holes – the 9th, a make-up par-3 of barely 100 yards, and the 13th, a par-5 so tight that you virtually have to walk up the fairway in single file.

Although it is festival season in Bavaria, I manage to miss most of the mayhem until my final port of call, the chic, quaint little town of Oberstaufen in a corner of Germany that bulges into Austria's roof. Our visit is timed to coincide with the Viehscheid, an annual ceremony to mark the bringing of the cows down from the hills for winter.

Dr Franz Berktold-Fackler is a small, lean man with a prim, short and exceptionally neat haircut. He's a director of tourism in the town and looks accustomed to being taken seriously. The trouble is that tight leather shorts revealing bony white legs make it hard to create a sensible first impression.

We arrive at the central marquee to find it packed with men of all shapes and sizes wearing exactly the same gear, and Franz visibly relaxes. Even the brass band wear their leder-hosen, while they crash out some thigh-slapping, tankard-brandishing oompah tunes.

"Ja, I've had these for 25 years and never washed them!" says Franz, pointing to his shorts and braces. Apparently, in many families such garments get handed down through the generations.

Oberstaufen is a thriving tourist town, full of quality hotels, good restaurants and its own extremely pleasant golf course. Like so many others in Bavaria it is a spa town, and used to be called Bad ('Bath') Oberstaufen until the council decided that sounded like a place for the elderly.

"We took the decision to drop the Bad because it didn't sound good," smiles Franz, obviously pleased with his English play on words.

While Bad Aibling has it's peat baths, Oberstaufen is known for the 'Schroth' dry diet treatment, an exercise in which the body is starved of liquid one day and then starved of food the next.

"It makes sense," explains Franz. "If a deer gets injured, knocked down by a car or something, it will stop drinking and eating until it is better. The body is left to concentrate on the injury rather than digesting food."

There are at least ten golf courses within an hour's drive of here, and one of them, Riefensberg, is across the border into Austria. It is quite a new facility, but one that is a good test for most players.

The clubhouse may be no more than a stone shell, but there are some good holes, especially those that follow the Weissach River.

To get the most from Bavaria, you need to prepare as much for the culture and the countryside as the golf. Near Oberstaufen, for instance, there is a chairlift that takes you to the top of the mountain, whence you can eavesdrop on a gathering of peaks from Germany, Austria and Switzerland.

Franz also recommends that I drop by Fussen on my way home, so that I can see the most famous of Ludwig's castles, Neuschwanstein. It stands like a Disney creation, all turrets and towers.

"You know, it took 14 carpenters four and a half years to do the wood carving in his bedroom," says Franz.

You know that you're in Bavaria when someone drinking Oktoberfest beer in leather shorts comes out with a statistic like that and it's true.

Lake Tegernseer. If your idea of post-golf heaven is lakes and mountains rather than sticky beaches, Bavaria could be for you.

THE NITTY GRITTY

Flights Lufthansa is offering a special deal from Stansted to Munich. Call 0049 180 3336633, or visit www.lufthansa.com.

Golf packages Moswin Tours, tel 0116 271 9922.

Where to stay Romantik Hotel Linder, Bad Aibling, call 0049 806190630.

Allgäuer Rosenalp, Oberstaufen, call 0049 838 67060.

Other courses Oberstaufen , call 0049 838 68529; Riefensberg , call 0043 551 38400.

More information German National Tourist Office, call 0207 317 0908; brochure line, call 09001 600 100.

The best of the courses

MAXLRAIN

7,068 yards, par 73
Call: 0049 806 11403.
■ A quality course which begins easily, but soon turns the screw. There are some excellent holes, of which the 4th and 5th stand out on the outward half. The 4th requires a precision drive to avoid thick woods tight to the left and a solitary tree in the fairway that threatens to stymie your approach. The 5th is a par-5 cutting through marshland, and demands some sensible course management if you are to avoid the reeds that border both sides of the fairway. Good placement is well rewarded on the 18th, which winds towards a clubhouse serving good food and beer.

MANGFALLTAL

6,723 yards, par 72
Call: 0049 806 36300.
■ The first nine here is set out in a fairly flat field, and at first appears to be a rather poor neighbour to the back nine, which twists and turns like a rollercoaster ride. Once you experience both, however, you might be tempted to say that the front nine is a greater and arguably more enjoyable test of golf. The homeward half is outrageous in design and at times even dangerous for the over-eager golfer. Cutting corners off doglegs, you are encouraged to hit blind over trees and greens that can be one or two holes ahead.

TEGERNSEER

6,002 yards, par 70
Call: 0049 802 28769.
■ This is an established club course and full of character – especially the first nine, which is probably the better of the two halves. Tegernseer gets off to an inspiring start with a long but wide par-4 followed by a par-5 that crosses a valley just short of the green. A number of holes here get the adrenalin pumping as you stand on the tee, and you can't really ask for much more than that. For those who like to take the driver from an elevated tee to a fairway that is way below, the 14th hole shouldn't disappoint.

Best kept secret

Swap your skis for your clubs
and have a memorable round
of golf…high up in the Alps!

olf in Austria has been one of the game's best kept secrets. But it's now set to become one of Europe's exciting new golf holiday destinations as word spreads that there is spectacular action to be found in the heart of the Alps. What Austria, you may ask yourself? After all, surely it's a country best known for its fabulous skiing and walking holidays. However, the country already boasts over 120 golf courses, with several more being planned for the future to meet the ever growing popularity in the sport.

Austrian golf offers an immediate difference. With courses being set in dramatic mountain surroundings, teeing off quite literally takes your breath away. That said, on a more practical note, the Austrian golf season only runs from late April to early October when average temperatures are in line with the rest of central Europe. But the benefit from the winter break when courses are closed because of snow cover, is that the quality of greens and fairways remain superb throughout the season.

With over 20 years experience specialising in winter and summer holidays in Austria, MW Golf, part of the Liberty Leisure Group, now present an exclusive range of bespoke golf holidays to the main golfing centres.

MW Golf's team of golfers have selected those top courses they rate as

being among many of the best in Europe. With several of these also employing English PGA professionals, standards are as high as one would expect throughout the world, and language barriers are never an obstacle.

And all the courses that feature in MW Golf's holiday programme are within a short drive away from your chosen hotel. Privately owned, these hotels offer comfortable surroundings, first-class facilities and excellent cuisine. More so,

being hands-on family run as is typical in Austria, you can be sure of enjoying a level of personal service, which is increasingly ignored by many hotels found in large golfing complexes.

Golf in the Alps will capture the imagination of those with the passion to discover new golfing experiences. With excellent courses, quality accommodation and outstanding value for money, as well as the stunning scenery, the game here is about to set new holiday standards

The championship course at Eichenheim is carved into the natural beauty of the mountains.

for the most discerning of golfers.

For more information about some of the key golfing courses in the provinces of Tirol, Salzburgerland and Carinthia, visit Golf Alpin's website on www.golf-alpin.at. They also offer an excellent discount card to use at any five of their affiliated golf courses giving reduced green fees.

Host to the PGA
Challenge Tour's
Austrian Championship.
That's Eichenheim.

Eichenheim
(Kitzbühel, Tirol)

Set among the magnificent alpine scenery of Kitzbühel, Eichenheim presents a real challenge for every golfer. Ranked in the top three courses in Austria, Eichenheim has become the home of the PGA Challenge Tour's Austrian Championship. The course, manicured from tee to superb undulating greens, is carved into the natural beauty of the mountains with cunningly positioned water to keep you thinking on every shot. After negotiating the magnificent outward nine you'll arrive via the frightening tenth and short eleventh on the tee of the signature twelfth. An awesome tee invites you to drive, and better make it straight, into the abyss, over a 200 ft precipice onto the fairway below.

■ For your accommodation, we can recommend the Hotel Rasmushof (www.rasmushof.at) centrally located in Kitzbühel. This hotel not only boasts excellent leisure facilities including an indoor pool but also its own 9-hole course. Three day packages including flights, transfers, B&B accommodation and two rounds of golf start at £399. Other recommended courses in the area include Schwarzsee, Kitzbühel, Kössen and the two courses at Zell am See.

■ MW Golf Team's verdict: "If, like us, you'd never considered playing golf in Austria, you will quite simply be amazed by Eichenheim. It's as good as any course we've played and we mean any course!"

Mondsee (Oberösterreich)

When we first brought our golfing experts to the Golf Club Am Mondsee they were fresh from playing a competition at Les Bordes, a course ranked as one of the best in Europe. After 18 holes here, they thought they were still in France. Except that the scenery was better! You will love every minute on this course. Even if your courage fails and you take the percentage shots over some of the water, there will be reward enough in making bogey, especially on the closing holes. Lush lake reeds abound around many greens and the prolific trees on every hole add to the enjoyment of the test. Walking off the 18th green we promise you'll want to play it again but stop awhile to enjoy the excellent clubhouse facilities and the familiar warm welcome from Willi Müller, the club manager.

■ Accommodation close to Mondsee would be the charming Hotel Hollweger in St.Gilgen, (www.hollweger.at) idyllically situated on the shores of Lake Wolfgang. Three day packages including flights, transfers, B&B accommodation and two rounds of golf start at £389. Other courses in the area include Eugendorf, Altentann and Bad Ischl.

■ MW Golf Team's verdict: "Demanding, exciting and beautiful, from every tee to every green you have to keep the concentration going. Mondsee is an absolute delight. Can we play it again please?"

Mondsee has to be seen to be believed...a well maintained course in great surroundings.

Water features strongly at Seltenheim.

"Seltenheim is a challenging blend of Scottish links and American parkland"

Seltenheim (Carinthia)

Klagenfurt provides the gateway to another feast of great golf courses in southern Austria, and Seltenheim, a few minutes from the airport, is the five-star main course! A challenging blend of the Scottish links and American parkland, the club manager and Director of Golf for the Carinthia Province, Oliver Pilloni and his team, have worked magic to produce a superb championship course. Undulating fairways and huge manicured greens, tactically placed around the magnificent lake, make Seltenheim unforgettable. It hosted the Austrian Amateur Championship and the International Matchplay Tournament 2001.

■ Stay at the Arcotel in Klagenfurt (www.arcotel.at) and combine your golf with a little culture in Klagenfurt when you're not playing. Three day packages including flights, transfers, B&B accommodation and two rounds of golf start at £325.

■ MW Golf Team's verdict: " We were amazed to discover that the course was opened as recently as 1997. It has the feel of a well established venue. Every hole offers a serious challenge to the serious golfer and you will have to be on top form with the putter to keep your card respectable. The fairways and greens are immaculate while the undulations will provide plenty of interesting lies for your approach shots. An excellent test of golf."

Hidden gems

Classic courses, stunning scenery, great hospitality ...Ireland has everything you could want from a golfing holiday.

There is one absolute "must do" pilgrimage any serious golfer must make before he or she tees off to that great pearly fairway in the sky. And that is a trip to Ireland where you'll find some of the most challenging and inspirational golf courses on earth. Legendary names in golf can be found here...Portmarnock, Ballybunion and Waterville in the south, and Royal County Down and Royal Portrush in the north. Their beauty and legend has attracted golfers from across the globe from US Presidents to movie stars...plus the odd major winner or two.

But because of their prestige and popularity, getting a tee time on one of these courses can be a difficult task.

Don't despair because hidden amongst the golfing greats there are many other treasured gems. Here we have picked out a selection that are well worth a visit.

Narin and Portnoo Golf Club is simply a fabulous place for a game, rain or shine. Built in 1930 the 18 holes are among the most natural you'll ever see and possibly the most fun you'll ever play. At a little under 6,000 yards, it does have a hard time foiling the single-figure man armed with a bulbous-headed titanium driver especially when the flags are hanging limp. But when the wind gets up no amount of titanium allows even the most able golfer the luxury of being able to relax. There are six picture book par threes and a profusion of thrilling two shotters all of which finish

The Island course near Dublin was voted 70th in the Golf World Top 100 rankings.

on small greens with silky putting surfaces.

But the best part is very few people from overseas have ever heard of the place. And even if those that have come without a detailed map of the area and a saint's patience, the narrow winding roads linking the N56 and the small village of Portnoo will most probably get the better of them and they'll turn back towards the main road scratching their heads. That means you either get the course to yourself or you share it with a few of the locals who, like most of their countrymen, have turned hospitality into an art form. We were made so welcome, the thought of turning down the invitation to stay on another day and play it again was never even considered.

And don't be thinking Portnoo is the only Irish jewel you're not familiar with. There are loads of courses you probably haven't heard of across the Irish Sea, which, if played once, would become regular hangouts.

Like Bundoran, 25 miles further south. It's another classic Irish course, part links and part inland, that has probably escaped the attention of all but the most intrepid of golfers. Designed in 1894 by GL Ballie and remodelled 33 years later by the great Harry Vardon, Bundoran is one of those venues you stumble upon quite by accident then make immediate plans for future visits. Christy O'Connor came here as head professional in 1951 and stayed for six years, a period he often referred to as one of the happiest of his life. He was particularly fond of the par four 17th, often hailed as the best hole on the course, although the long par threes have their share of admirers.

Another remodelled and largely undiscovered west coast diamond can be found in the village of Enniscrone 35 miles to the west of Bundoran, in County Sligo. After a humble beginning in 1918 when only a modest nine holes existed, the course was extended in 1974 by Ireland's greatest home-grown architect Eddie Hackett who utilised the formidable dunes to great effect. Donald Steel recently added three new holes and with the reclamation of six old holes Enniscrone is now a 27-hole complex which one visitor to the club's website declared "the greatest in the world".

Perhaps he hadn't been to Carne Golf Links on the far west tip of County Mayo. Another Hackett masterpiece, this course is the new home of the Belmullet Golf Club and opened in 1992. Carne is now a familiar name in most golfing circles but its remoteness ensures it stays relatively quiet, even during the summer months. Hackett, a modest man by nature, was so pleased with the end result he even allowed himself a pat on the back. "I am thrilled with the way the course has turned out," he said. "And I reiterate my opinion that ultimately there might be no better links golf course in the country nor I doubt anywhere." Jim Engh, one of America's most acclaimed designers of recent years, agreed paying it the ultimate compliment of ranking it alongside Ballybunion and Pebble Beach.

Shifting over to the east coast, your first stop, if you want to avoid the crowds of the more famous venues, should be Arklow Golf Club, an hour or so south of Dublin in County Wicklow. After discovering this is yet another Hackett design you won't be at all surprised to find a course of such beauty or one so challenging, despite the fact it tops out at a meagre 5,770 yards.

Half an hour the other side of the capital lies the fabulous Laytown and Bettystown GC, Des Smyth's home course. Originally laid out in 1909 on a narrow strip of duneland, it can be an extremely tough course if the weather is anything other than clement. Smyth has made recent alterations to the 6th and 7th holes, making the front nine even more testing.

Ardglass Golf Club in County Down is undergoing some changes of its own, with three new holes opening in 2003, but it already ranks in most people's Irish Top 20. Some of the holes, especially those that hug the coastline like the short 2nd, are absolutely stunning and will linger in the memory long after you've left. The Mountains of Mourne come into sight from the 3rd tee and while not quite as conspicuous as they are at Royal County Down, they still contribute to a wonderful vista.

There are dozens more courses in Ireland you won't have read about that are worth hopping on an aeroplane or ferry for. The Island, just north of Dublin, was rated 70th best course in the British Isles by Golf World recently and is certainly worth a visit. Then there's Kirkistown Castle in County Down; Ballycastle and Bushfoot in Antrim; Castlerock in Londonderry offering 27 holes of classic links golf, running alongside the River Bann; Connemara in Galway; Ballyliffin's 36 holes of links; County Donegal and the magical Cruit Island in Donegal.

Travel south and one of the newer developments is Seafield, located in Ballymoney, Co Wexford. Here, Peter McEvoy, former Walker Cup captain, has created a mix of parkland, heathland and seaside holes on a cliff top location. Just further down the road is Courtown, a quintessential parkland course created in an old country estate which also has wonderful views of the sea and a number of quite memorable par three holes.

With the ferry teminal at Rosslare offering a perfect starting point for a visit to the sunniest part of Ireland, you won't have to travel too far to find top class courses. Rosslare is a lovely links located on a sandy peninsula while St Helen's Bay barely a 10-minute drive from the port, overlooks the St George's Channel.

Dungarvan in Co Waterford has much to offer, including three golf courses – Gold Coast, Dungarvan and West Waterford. All of which makes for as good a reason as any to use it as an ideal touring base for the south coast with courses in the Cork area – including Fota Island, Harbour Point, Lee Valley, Little Island and the Old Head – all worth visits that will make you yearn for a return.

The European is one of the most stunning layouts in the whole of Ireland.

Enniscrone is finally getting noticed...it's just made Golf World's Top 100 courses list.

Stay in the cities and play the top courses

One way of sampling the delights of Irish golf is to stay in one of the many bustling cities and play courses within the catchment area. For instance, Dublin, Belfast, Limerick and Cork all offer an abundance of superb golf and a welcome from the friendliest people in the world.

COURSES NEAR DUBLIN
You've hardly stepped off the plane before you come face-to-face with St Margaret's Golf Club – a most welcoming, friendly and surprisingly peaceful parkland course set on the airport's perimeter. Head a little way up the road and you'll find the Portmarnock Hotel, the former summer home of the Jameson whiskey family, with stunning links golf course designed by Bernhard Langer. Neighbouring Portmarnock Golf Club has hosted top class events

such as the Walker Cup and The Irish Open. And 45 minutes north of the airport are the championship links of Seapoint's 7,000-yarder, whose closing holes all edge alongside the sea, and County Louth (Baltray) Golf Club.

City West Golf Club and the K Club, host to the 2006 Ryder Cup, are also surprisingly close to the capital, along with another classy newcomer in the shape of Carton House.

South of Dublin, towards the little seaside town of Greystones, lies Druid's Glen with its newly opened Marriott Hotel, Powerscourt, Glen of the Downs and Pat Ruddy's The European, a Golf World Top 100 course and one of the most unpretentious and stunning links layouts. For more information on city breaks visit www.visitdublin.com

COURSES NEAR BELFAST
Close to the city there are superb parkland layouts such as Harry S Colt's Royal Belfast, the oldest club in Ireland, built in 1881 and one of three Royal courses in Northern Ireland, the others being Portrush and County Down. Another Colt creation is to be enjoyed at Belvoir Park along with such leafy classics as Shandon Park and Malone's 18 and nine-hole layouts. Close to Belfast International Airport, lies the Hilton Templepatrick, which offers an 18-hole golf course, golf academy and a superb range of practice and leisure facilities. Mount Ober Golf Club, south east of the city, not only offers 18 holes of golf and a golf academy, but also a dry ski slope and toboggan run. Green fees range from a modest £20 to £40 for 18 holes. There are 9 nine-hole golf courses in and

around Belfast, including Ormeau and Colin Valley where you can enjoy a quick round and a pint or two in the clubhouse for under £20. Two of the world's greatest links courses are an easy drive from Belfast city – these hardly need an introduction but are Tom Morris's Royal County Down and another Colt classic at Royal Portrush. For more information visit www.gotobelfast.com

Courses near Cork

Cork Golf Club is a parkland layout designed by Alistair McKenzie and enjoys the picturesque setting of the River Lee's estuary. Water also plays an important part at Fota Island, another lovely parkland course a short drive from the city. Fota Island has twice hosted the Murphy's Irish Open, the Irish Amateur Open and the Irish PGA Championship and her fairways have been trodden by many top players including Padraig Harrington, Colin Montgomerie and Paul McGinley. More parkland golf is on offer at Lee Valley Golf Club, which enjoys a rolling layout with panoramic views set against a dramatic backdrop of hills and mountains. You can also play what is called the West Cork Circuit taking in

five courses – Skibbereen, Celtic Ross, Kinsale Golf Club, Bandon and Berehaven. For more information visit www.corkkerry.ie

Courses near Limerick

Shannon Golf Club was designed by Commander John Harris and stands next to the international airport with which both the club and the river, the latter of which has to be carried on the par three 17th, share their names. Despite boasting a super parkland layout, those Atlantic winds can rip across this fairways in the colder months giving it a links feel. Limerick Golf Club boasts a golfing pedigree stretching back over 100 years and its tree-lined fairways measure 6,400 yards. Ryder Cup player Des Smyth designed the very attractive Limerick County Golf and Country Club and its wooded and rolling fairways have attracted many admirers to the set-up, which includes excellent practice facilities, teaching academy and self-catering cottages. Adare Manor is a real treat for anyone wishing to combine a stately manor house with Ireland's only Trent Jones-designed golf course. And we mustn't rest here without mentioning Dromoland Castle, another five-star

"The really hot new story is Doonbeg, the Greg Norman links course set on a dune lined bay north of Shannon"

hotel and golf course, although the golf course is undergoing considerable refurbishment and won't be re-opened until 2003. However, the really hot new story about these parts is Doonbeg, the Greg Norman-designed links course set on a crescent shaped sandy, dune-lined bay north of the Shannon. For more information visit www.shannondev.ie

Doonbeg on the west coast of Ireland, spectacularly designed by Greg Norman.

The splendid K Club is getting ready for the Ryder Cup in 2006.

The Greatest Golf Show on Earth

HAVING BEEN PUT back a year, the K Club is already streets ahead with its plans to host the Ryder Cup on its acclaimed Arnold Palmer course and on Irish soil for the first time. What perhaps is surprising is that this competition has taken so long to arrive in Ireland. After all, Irish players have been part of Ryder Cup teams since the legendary Fred Daly was selected in 1947. A total of 15 top Irish professionals have notched up Ryder Cup honours, including Christy O'Connor Senior, Eamonn Darcy, Des Smyth, Padraig Harrington and in 2002, the K Club's own touring professional, Paul McGinley, joined this distinguished list to great acclaim.

Paul himself and the K Club's golf director, Paul Crowe, know just how much detailed planning, hard work and millions of pounds worth of development money are being invested in the K Club's Straffan home just south-west of Dublin's bustling city centre. Paul Crowe commented: "What is so exciting about the Ryder Cup coming to Ireland is that it will bring a great celebration of Irishness. Because there is so much to see and do, it will be a great Irish party."

By the time 2006 spins around there will be many changes to the club, the hotel and the course itself. Some of these alterations, such as the IR£12 million investment in the hotel, have already happened, notably an entire new wing.

The Ryder Cup is a great event for spectators, and course routing is to be altered to improve access and viewing for the crowds and the media. It's a bit complicated but basically the current back eight holes will switch places with the front eight holes to create a completely new layout with only the original ninth hole and the superb 18th finishing hole remaining in their original spot.

Finishing touches are being made to the new linksy-style Palmer South Course on 170 acres across from the existing 8th and 16th greens on the opposite side of the River Liffey, which winds through the existing course. When the 7200-yard course opens for play in July 2003, this new addition will give the K Club a 36-hole complex which will not only benefit visitors but provide a useful addition to Ryder Cup plans.

It will be tested to the full the following year and again in 2005 when, subject to European Tour approval, the action for the Smurfit European Open tees off on this exciting new layout. Figures for this work must be mind-boggling. It's not only the millions of noughts on the cheques and extra staff and hours, but also things like one million cubic metres of earth being excavated for ponds and contouring; elevations some 30 feet in height plus extensive bunkering being created and gallons of water for water hazards. As part of the IR£12 million golf spend, there's a new clubhouse to be opened, a conference centre to be inaugurated and a blue ribbon waiting to be cut to hail the opening of a splendid new leisure centre.

Ireland's K Club was already prominent on the golfing map of the world. Ryder Cup 2006 will be the golf party of a lifetime. One not to be missed!

The Dubliners

Four 5-star courses in Ireland are just one hour from Dublin.

Once upon a time it used to be that to be afforded respect, importance and success, any self-respecting popular beat combo had to be called "The" something or other. Hence The Beatles, The Rolling Stones, The Who and The Beach Boys. They sound definitive, have gravitas, they shout that they are the official, original and best version and that all other soundalikes and lookalikes are to be avoided. It had to stop, of course, when some smart Alecs called themselves The The. But what many rock and rollers don't realise is that we golfers started this trend 105 years ago when The New Course was built at St Andrews and the original course became The Old Course.

While music has largely turned its back on the "The" phenomenon, it is still all the rage in the more laid-back world of golf. Moving up the Top 100 pop charts around Dublin are The Island, The European, The K Club and Druids Glen. Well, there's always someone who has to be different.

The K in K Club stands for Kildare, and the suggestion is that this is the definitive club in the county. In fact there are at least a dozen and the K Club isn't even the oldest. It is only 11 years old but is already The Ryder Cup course for Ireland in 2006 thanks largely to the deep pockets of the Smurfit family who made their millions in the packaging industry. Armed with this knowledge, you anticipate grandeur when you turn into

Words **Paul Mahoney**   Photography **Angus Murray**

The European club. Hard to believe it's just 10 years old.

"The River Liffey sparkles and bubbles along the left of

this exclusive country club environment – and it delivers. You can smell the lush green grass of the fairways and perfectly manicured greens alongside the road as you drive past the Brideshead Revisited-style hotel and on to the clubhouse. And you can smell the money. It makes you feel special, successful, rich, a mover and shaker. Pity then that, as a visitor, you are brought down to earth by the sign sending you off to the car park for the great unwashed 400 yards from the members' cars conveniently parked in their reserved bays in front of the clubhouse.

Signs on the tees also split members and visitors but, if you ask, they are happy for you to play off any tee you like. You will be happy, too, to discover that the army of pros, assistants and bar staff have all graduated from the University of American-style service-with-a-smile –

but with quieter and more lyrical accents. The American theme continues. Since Arnold Palmer is the course designer, this is not surprisingly an American target golf experience – without the weather – laid out over mature Irish parkland.

Man-made mounds add definition to contoured greens and clusters of wide bunkers while corporate societies and American tourists hole out for 12s in a buggy environment that ensures you will probably have to endure the dreaded five-hour round. Lucky, then, that the drinks cart – presumably introduced to make our cousins from across the Pond feel at home – pops up at regular intervals to keep golfers fed and watered and alive. Like its Ryder Cup peers – the Brabazon Course at The Belfry and the Wentwood Hills Course at Celtic Manor – many of the holes at The K Club,

although all sprinkled with TLC, merge into the okay but forgettable category. They largely make up the maths on the scorecard between the memorable and the spectacular. Its wow factor hits you at the double dogleg par five 7th. The River Liffey sparkles and bubbles along left of the fairway then curls in to create an island green. The river stays for the 8th, daring you to take the Tiger line over the corner. The backdrop of the palatial hotel to your right ensures this corner of the K Club is the talking point back in the bar.

The 537-yard 18th is reachable in two but, as Padraig Harrington will testify after the European Open here in July, the water left and in front of the green comes into play. The K Club is simply a course waiting to be famous. Not in a Muirfield or a St Andrews or a Royal Birkdale kind of way but in a unique Ryder Cup way.

the fairway, ensuring this spot is the most talked about"

The 7th, 8th, 16th and 18th are sleeping giants. Prepare for them to be awoken in September 2006 to make or break legends and create golf history. You have four years to play them before the green fee rockets even more.

The Island sounds like an arrogant boast that this is the only course on the island of Ireland worth playing. In fact, this is a shy old links that has been hiding in the shadows of its wealthier and more famous Portmarnock neighbour across the estuary since 1890. Back then, the only way to reach the course, to avoid an arduous trip around the coast, was by boat. Hence its name. There is no sign of splendour or lavish money gestures here. Polite nods and smiles and "how are ya, fellas?" abound. The atmosphere feels like a quiet village club rather than a corporate country club. It is a pleasant shock to find an unassuming hidden away

Golf World Top 100 course. Airs and graces are not required. Golfers can park together, change in the same locker room and drink in the bar. A welcome socialist democratic society at work – if not a very social one. Apres golfers could be counted on one hand. This is clearly not the place to hang around. Perhaps it could be down to the musty stench in the bar. Maybe the carpet needs changing.

Out on the course it feels like you have been thrown back in time. This is how golf must have felt like 112 years ago when this links opened for business. This is no-nonsense golf taken neat, without ice or a mixer. The fairways are hard and fast and scruffy and look like they have been gorged out of the earth between scraggy sand dunes with a blunt trowel. And that's a compliment. The greens are sloping and huge and downhill putts are impossible to lag, let alone hole. The

wind changes direction more often than an ambitious politican and the whole experience is marvellous – if your ego and handicap can take the lashing.

You'll never forget the closing five. The 14th hugs the estuary filled with yachts and boats in the marina. Its fairway is the narrowest I have ever seen. Stand on the tee, hold your arms out at shoulder width. The space you have to hit is the distance between your hands. Terrifying. Out of sight of the clubhouse, a five-ball of Americans (must they do everything bigger than the rest of us?) were pretending to have fun orienteering the dunes while even they couldn't be heard in the amphitheatre of peace and tranquillity of the 15th and 16th. The Island is probably the greatest course you've never heard of.

The European is a lofty and rather daft title but one which must be swallowed with a large dollop of fun and devilry. "It'll help the Americans find us," grins Pat Ruddy, the course owner, architect and professional Mickey-taker. Tiger Woods found it in July along with Mark O'Meara and their travelling Californian Circus on the now traditional pre-Open Irish tour. Ruddy's dream is to host the Open if the R&A ever take it back to Ireland. But for now his motto is golf for golf's sake and a doffed cap to less hurried times when access to the links was easy and relaxed. And it works.

One American visitor enthused that the course was "wunerful – every hole was sooo different." "Damn," Ruddy replied, deadpan, "I was trying to make them all exactly the same." Marvellous. You might even say Ruddy marvellous. But don't let this flippancy detract from the fact that this is a seriously spectacular links – and that American really was speaking sense. There is not a single hole that disappoints. Another American (don't you just love them) came puffing in to the clubhouse to explain that he had sliced into the Irish Sea from the 13th tee

THE ISLAND
The best course you've
never heard of.

and wondered where he should take a drop. "Wales," was Ruddy's reply. "But no nearer the hole." Americans who faint at the very thought of the coastline-hugging holes of Pebble Beach will require smelling salts from the 12th to the 15th at The European. But there is more to the course than merely staggering ocean views and whirling double greens. Raised tees give the whole experience a stadium feel that would embarrass the marketing men who coined the phrase "theatre of dreams" to describe a mere football pitch in Manchester.

Fairways weave their way between giant dunes and dense marram, their snaking shapes defined by sharply cut slopes as if lovingly knifed by an artist in a watercolour painting. Smooth rolling greens, a pleasure to three-putt, melt away into the rough via subtle first and second cuts. Attention to detail in the course is outstanding. Which is why the clubhouse is little more than a few tables and chairs. "Nobody travels to play a clubhouse," Ruddy smiles, saying he

knows the next project will be to build a clubhouse to match the splendour of the course. The European is only 10 years old but it feels like a veteran.

Druids Glen may well regret failing to prefix their course's name with the noble "The" word. It leaves a hole in the market in this glen for a band of ambitious druids. But they'll have some way to go topple the majesty of this seven-year-old parkland layout cocooned inside the 400-year-old Woodstock Estate.

There's a feel-good American flavour when you arrive at the grand mansion clubhouse built in 1770. Staff buzz around smiling and welcoming and making sure you have everyone you want and know where everything is. Trolleys are free – and you should take one for there are backbreaking hills – and a drinks and food buggy patrols the course. All this makes you feel you are an important customer getting value for money rather than just another ker-ching on the pro shop till.

There are plenty of water hazards

"This is how golf must have felt like over a
hundred years ago. It's no nonsense golf taken neat,
without ice or a mixer"

"Play challenging courses, relax and have fun...that's the
theme of golf around Dublin. It's a unique experience"

sprinkled across the course and it has hosted the Irish Open and the Seve Trophy, so you might expect to find an army of Americans taking time out from searching for their ancestry to play European tour championship venues. And they'd get the real deal, too, because you are allowed to tee up from the back tees at just over 7,000 yards. But this is very much an Irish experience – only seven per cent of visitors are from the United States; 80 percent are Irish and the rest from the mainland.

The course manager, apparently, is a seven-day workaholic. Bad news for Mrs Course Manager but great news for golfers for there are perfect lies from his Axminster-like fairways and the beautifully-cut greens make you feel you can hole out from anywhere. You can't, obviously. Landing areas are often generous and raised tees encourage you to open the shoulders and rip a driver. The par three 12th pays homage to its Augusta national counterpart with a stone bridge over a pond, large bunker on the left and a bank of flowers forming an aesthetic backdrop. From there, you climb to the 13th tee and the scene below looks like it has had a visit from Charlie and Alan Titchmarsh and their Ground Force team: flora, fauna, water features and stunning vistas. The island 17th – the last of the memorable short holes – is protected by a bunker shaped as wide as a clown's grin. The only thing to do when you underclub into the water is laugh. And that seems to be the theme of golf around Dublin – play challenging courses, relax and have fun. Strangely, Dublin has an advantage, here, over its rivals and it is mostly down to marketing. Dublin is a happy feel-good name, like chocolate, sand or jelly. You'll probably have just as fine a time in Skegness, Cleethorpes or Blackpool but it doesn't sound like you will. And I haven't even mentioned Guinness.

Go West!

Classic courses, stunning scenery, unbeatable hospitality… Ireland's South West has everything you could want from a golfing holiday. We look at two different holiday breaks.

Words: **Anne Harper**   Photography: **Allsport**

There are two absolutely "must do" pilgrimages any serious golfer must make before he or she tees off to that great pearly fairway in the sky. After Scotland's St Andrews, a very close matched golfing rite of passage has to be made to Ireland's stunningly beautiful South-West coast.

This romantic coastline, washed by the Atlantic seaboard and the warming Gulf Stream, has some of the most challenging and inspirational golf courses on earth. Legendary names in golf can be found here…Ballybunion, Waterville and Dingle, all created from unspoilt natural linksland. Their beauty and legend has attracted golfers from across the globe from US Presidents to movie stars... plus the odd major winner or two.

Shannon is the gateway to a lush green region of outstanding beauty. You can head south into Kerry or north towards Galway and everywhere you will find that uniquely Irish experience to visitors, which comes with friendliness, warmth and unstinting hospitality. The old advice "Go West"

has never been more appropriate. Accommodation is plentiful and can be as simple or as grand as you like – from castles and manor houses to luxury hotels and self-catering lodges or welcoming B&B and homely farmhouses. Getting there has never been easier either with a good selection of airlines – including the low cost options – and highly modern and superbly equipped ferries.

US Masters and Open champion Mark O'Meara is a huge fan of this part of Ireland and has made many visits, most notably with Tiger and the late Payne Stewart. His great-grandfather emigrated to Boston from south west Ireland and Mark's father declares it his favourite place in the world.

So what is it that makes it so special? "I have to say that it's a combination of everything," says O'Meara. "The country, the golf, the people.

"We have travelled around and played several of the courses – including Waterville and Ballybunion – and everywhere we went we just had such a warm welcome. That's what makes it so special."

Ballybunion...the jewel in South West Ireland's crown.

What to see, which places to visit, where to play

South West Ireland isn't just about great golf. Neither is it just the stunning scenery which makes this region such a special place to visit. There is also plenty to explore from picturesque villages to busy market towns and lovely cities like Limerick, which you will be relieved to note, is far removed from the image depicted in the recent movie Angela's Ashes.

MAP ILLUSTRATION: GRAHAM CACHES

Cliffs of Moher

■ The stunning **Cliffs of Moher** rise over 700 feet high and stretch for five miles along the coastline. They offer an ideal vantage point for cliff-top walks and watching the sun set over the Atlantic Ocean.

Irish music

■ The South West is one of the main areas for traditional Irish music. The pretty fishing village of Ballyvaughan on Galway Bay is a great place for a warm welcome and a warmer glass of something else.

Limerick & Galway

■ Limerick is good place to shop, to eat in its many restaurants and make new friends in its welcoming bars. The city is dominated by a mighty 13th century **St John's Castle,** which is always worth a visit. If it's just pure fun you're looking for, Galway's the place to be. It bustles and crackles all year round with some great event or activity. These range from a Literary Festival, a Jazz Festival, which attracts some of the big names, and the absolutely manic **Galway Races** in July.

The Burren

■ The Burren in County Clare is a spectacular West of Ireland offering. It consists of a vast area of limestone, and this unique landscape provides a home for a wide variety of fauna and flora.

River Shannon

■ There is cruising on the River Shannon – one of Europe's most attractive waterways – and dolphin watching off the Atlantic coast.

Bunratty Castle

■ There are many magnificent castles in this area to visit. At Bunratty you'll receive a lesson in Irish hospitality. Try one of Kathleen's Irish Nights at the Bunratty Castle Hotel – open every night and featuring Irish dancers and singers.

Ennis Town

■ Lovely little Ennis town is good for a pottering kind of outing with its lively pubs and restaurants. Close to the town is the **Biddy Early Brewery,** which is Ireland's first pub-brewery, and guided tours are on offer as well as tastings of such award winning beers as Black Biddy and Real Biddy. Still on the booze theme, a visit to the **Bunratty Mead and Liqueur Co** gives a "lesson on how the Irish make celebration and warm hospitality a national treasure."

Blarney Stone

■ A trip to Cork is well worth it, even if it's just for a trip to the Blarney Stone. Kissing the stone is supposed to give the kisser the gift of winning persuasiveness (blarney). It's tough to reach the stone – it's between the main castle wall and the parapet. Kissers have to lie on their back and bend backward, holding iron bars for support.

Tralee is another course for the golfing purist.

HOLIDAY 1 If you want...
A break for the golf purist

I am quite selective about where I play my golf and I want to book just the top courses on the West Coast. What are they?
The most famous is Ballybunion, which attracts all the US celebrities and top golfers, followed by Tralee and Waterville. There's the spectacular new Greg Norman designed links course at Doonbeg which opens in July and looks set to be the rising star. But don't forget, there are other excellent courses – both links and parkland, which are not so well known and offer an excellent test of golf.

So how can I book a tee time?
You can't directly! Ballybunion is almost fully booked from one year to the next. Members get first pick, and then there are the bookings by golf societies. The tour operators block book the rest, which leaves very little for anyone else. Tralee is also very difficult to get on and Waterville is restricted too.

Why has this happened?
These courses have attracted some of the world's top players like Mark O'Meara, Tom Watson and Tiger Woods. Such popularity, whilst putting this area of Ireland on the world golfing map, also brings its own problems and – despite the impact of September 11th - they are still fully booked up until winter.

So what do you suggest I do?
Your best bet is to talk to one of the UK-based specialist operators who will have pre-booked tee times at courses as part of their packages. But if you want to enjoy a golfing break under your own steam this summer consider some top class alternatives.

So let's name some alternatives.
Well if it's links golf you're looking for, there's Killarney, Lahinch, Dooks and Dingle, plus Doonbeg,

INSIDER'S TIP:
Although there is plenty of variety on offer when it comes to golf courses, it pays to play one venue more than once.

but that doesn't open officially until July 1st. Superb parkland options include Shannon, Killeen and Drumoland.

But aren't they just B list clubs – Division One as opposed to Premier League?
Don't even think it! These are top courses. It is said that Doonbeg, north of Shannon, has absorbed Greg Norman's every waking moment for the past few years, but it is set to very rapidly become one of the great links courses in the most magical setting. It has 18 holes of unspoilt links golf played across towering sand dunes, on a crescent shaped bay in a much contested conservation area, and every effort has been made to protect this beautiful setting.

Dingle is equally beautiful in setting and thrilling in nature while boasting of being the most westerly golf club in Europe, and Lahinch's Old Course was laid

down by none other than Old Tom Morris himself followed up by later alterations by Dr Alastair McKenzie.

Do I have to take a caddie?
You don't have to take anything, but most clubs can arrange for caddies and it's part of the Irish golfing experience. Apart from which your caddie's intimate knowledge of the course and his observations on life and the universe will prove to add a memorable aspect to your round.

Wild and rugged, Waterville is traditionally ranked in the Golf World Top 100 Courses.

If you want...
The ideal short break

We're a mixed group of golfers – husbands and wives, who want to relax, and sample the craic. Where's the best place to be?
All points of the compass around Shannon add up to this magic mixture and we would bet diamonds that you can't fail to enjoy yourselves, but here's a couple of suggestions. For some luxury self-catering try Limerick County Golf and Country Club's four-star holiday cottages right beside the first tee. Or for a romantic stay in an Irish castle try Dromoland Castle, ten miles from Shannon in County Clare. It's set in 400 acres, offers 75 luxury bedrooms, an Egon Ronay restaurant and beautifully laid out golf course meandering through richly wooded grounds.

I am looking for a genuine Irish experience. Where's a good place to find a welcoming bar?
Everywhere. But if you head for Killarney you'll find lots of bars where you'll experience great hospitality. O'Laurie's in the High Street is the place to down a few pints of the black stuff and revel in the warmth and wit of the regulars

What about the golf away from the classic courses.
Try the Nines of Kerry – eight delightful nine-hole golf courses, which will give you an enjoyable few days of golf at a price that won't damage your wallet. Each course has two tees and is built to championship standards. They are: Ardfert, Ballybeggan, Ballyheigue, Castlegregory, Dunloe, the Kerries, Listowel and Ross – hardly household golfing names but worthy of inclusion.
If you want to try links golf, the Castle Course at Lahinch is a challenging prospect.

We want to play at least one serious round of links golf plus a

pretty testing parkland option. Any suggestions?
Lahinch's Old Course is a classic test of links golf and is a par 72, 6,753-yard cracker designed to test even the best golfer. Its most notorious hole is the par five 5th known as the Klondyke where you have to play over a deep sand dune wall to a blind green. If it's parkland, then Shannon has been the choice of many top golfers such as Seve, Nick Faldo and Greg Norman. Water features on a number of holes and strategically placed bunkers and wind from the estuary can make this very tough indeed.

INSIDER'S TIP:
Ask your travel agent for advice about arranging your tee times for you. It takes away the hassle.

To be honest we're only staying for a few days and want to play golf and see a few sights too
There are some fine clubs within a short drive of Shannon. Ennis Golf Club at Drumbiggle and a fairly new club at Woodstock are both superb and mature parkland courses. The PGA European Tour has used East Clare Golf Club as a venue for its Irish Seniors Open in 1998 when it was less than two years old. Bright and breezy seaside golf can be found at Kilkee and Kilrush Golf Clubs while further along the coastline is Spanish Point Golf Club which enjoys a lovely setting above the Shannon estuary.

When is the best time of year to take a short break?
Golf courses and accommodations start to get busy from early April and remain that way through until October. However, July is an excellent time to visit as most golfers are off on their main family holidays then and you'll find the courses less busy.

And is midweek better than a weekend?
It has to be said that a midweek break is much better any time of the year as the courses are busy with members at the weekends.

A tee time at 2am! Are you nuts?

THE SUNDANCE KID
It's Round One and it's night-time? Or is it daytime? Anyone got the right time?

The Finnish word 'Hullu' looks and sounds like it might be a friendly welcome. Instead it describes, in the nicest possible way of course, the behaviour of our European cousins. Hullu means crazy – and it captures perfectly the spirit of the Midnight Sun 90-hole Marathon tournament which takes place near the home of Santa Claus. Hullu.

It is played on a course in Finnish Lapland that is now cloaked in snow, where the temperature can plummet to minus 40°C, and where there is only daylight for about as long as it takes to boil an egg. Desperate winters shroud the forest and fields bringing golf to a standstill for six months.

So when the snow and ice melts and the sun begins to breathe life back into the grass, those mad Lapps are chomping at the bit to smack that little white ball around. And, of course, as mid summer approaches the sun stays in the skies for longer and longer until it hangs there above the firs and teeming salmon rivers for 24 hours a day. That is why the trend for midnight marathons has come to be a part of Finnish golfing culture.

I flew in to Kemi, the gateway to Lapland and within two hours our team of nutters had checked in, and the first pair was standing on the 1st tee of the Green Zone Golf Club in Tornio for a Texas scramble. It was 7.30 on a balmy evening. Barmy more like.

Green Zone is unique because it is the only course in the world that straddles two nations sitting as it does across the border of Finland and Sweden, with six and half greens in Finland and 11 and a half in Sweden. It is also the only course I have played where water comes into the reckoning on 16 of the holes, and some of it puts the fear of God into you. It might also hold the record for the largest mosquitos in Christendom. We got round to the toughest stretch of holes from 11 to13 just as the beasts were at their feistiest. They were as large as humming birds, and as hungry as bears. Trying to hit a cultured draw with the insect Luftwaffe whizzing around your temples is a taxing business. We crossed the bridge from Sweden back into Finland by the 18th green at just before

Those golf crazy people among you would love to be able to play 24 hours a day, right? And where there's a will, there's a tee time any time you like.

Words: **Steve Carr** Photography: **Angus Murray**

midnight, a little spottier than before but invigorated. I kept on thinking that the sun was about to dip below the horizon, and darkness would come, but it didn't and it wouldn't for some weeks yet.

One round down, four to go. As we took a beer to the sauna we checked when our next tee time was – 6am. I got to bed at 1.30 and the sun was still firing its rays through the cracks in my blackout curtains. It was 30°C in the room, because the sun had been browbeating my window non-stop now for three weeks. Sleep was difficult to come by. I could not get the room dark and I was glowing like plutonium. A 5.15 alarm call was almost welcome just so I could get out into the freshness of morning.

Ted, another of my team-mates who had just finished the graveyard shift having teed off at 11.30 at night, handed over our car keys as we looked at each other through the slits that were our eyes. The temperature gauge in reception read 21.7°C.

Waiting for us on the tee were Matti and Pekka, who had finished their first round only three hours ago. Already I knew when the border crossings came. The first time is at the 3rd when you drive across a band of water from a Finnish tee to a Swedish fairway. But stranger still was when my partner Christer teed off on the par-3 6th at 7.35am and sunk his birdie putt at 8.39. The hole is not so long or difficult to warrant that much time to be taken, but instead the green is split in two by the

NO SLEEP TIL YOU FINNISH
Crister, Seppo, Ted and Golf World's 4-handicapper.

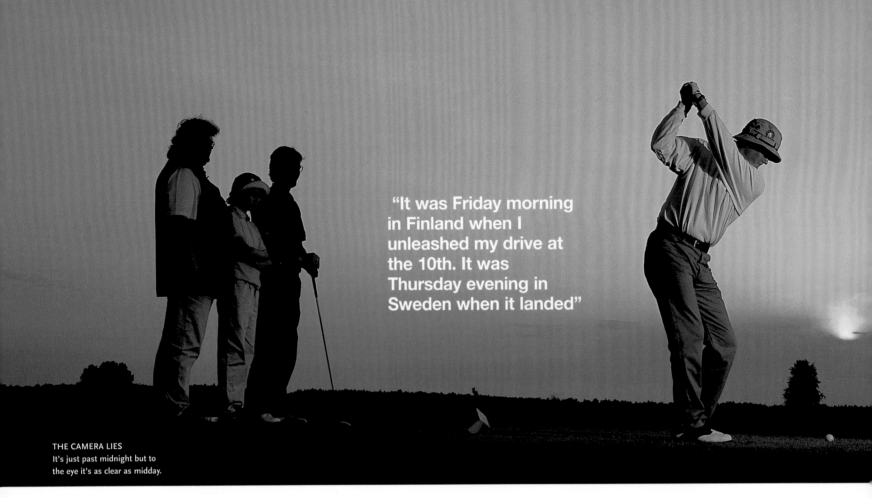

"It was Friday morning in Finland when I unleashed my drive at the 10th. It was Thursday evening in Sweden when it landed"

THE CAMERA LIES
It's just past midnight but to the eye it's as clear as midday.

BORDER PATROL
Six and a half greens are layed out in Finland, 11 and a half in Sweden's time zone.

border line and each half is in a different time zone.

And time was what it was all about – trying to adjust to it, that is. And still the sun was up there smiling. That fact was rammed home when I urged on the fourball in front of us with the words: "If they don't hurry up we'll be here until the sun comes down." Christer quite rightly pointed out that he doubted it since it would next set on August the 9th. It was June 28.

For us, we now had our longest gap between rounds, and already I was feeling the pinch of fatigue, which could only get worse with our 10.30 evening tee time. I did try and get some shut-eye in the afternoon after another burn in the sauna back at our hotel, but a couple of hours was all I could manage in the extraordinary heat and arctic light. We were only 100km south of the Arctic Circle but it was 25°C outside.

More joy at the 10th tee on Round Three. I may not have had a hole-in-one, nor won The Open, but I have toyed with time and turned back the clock. It was Friday morning when I unleashed my drive. It was Thursday evening when it landed. That is some golfing feat not

even the god-like Tiger Woods has done. I would love to claim it was so powerful it travelled faster than the speed of light, but instead it was 12.30am Finnish time when I teed off and 11.30pm and 7 seconds when it bounced in Sweden.

It was a bizarre but cheery moment and especially good timing as we approached Amen Corner, nicknamed so because of the combination of treacherous forested holes and the flying squad that loitered baying for your blood. That night the holes were still as tough but the mosquitos less of a threat. I have a feeling that they'd sucked all the goodness out of me the night before, or it might have been the use of Christer's unique repellent. During dinner he had let me into his secret. "The best way I find is to drink beer." Very Finnish. I couldn't work out if the local brew Lapin Kulta (Lapland Gold) contained a chemical that mozzies hated or simply that your pain and suffering went away the more you drank. But it had been worth a try.

Our flagging party reached the sanctuary of the clubhouse at 2.45am. I sat in quiet contemplation of the last 30

hours' events. This is a unique event going on non-stop for almost 100 hours, but the novelty could wear a little thin on a course that is under ice for six months a year if it wasn't such a strange and incomparable event. I was experiencing a kind of golfing jetlag – not necessarily totally physical because it was mentally warping too thanks to the bewildering tee times.

All those tour pros that complain about unsociable start times should try this. Here you can't even protest about having to get up at the crack of dawn. There isn't one.

We snatched a few hours rest before catching the last few minutes of breakfast and then it was back to the links to play with Pontus and Pentti at 11am. By now the tricky and idiosyncratic course was growing on me. It needed patience, exact ball striking and a good deal of luck to tackle its watery charms. This was a tough test for sure, and after that round while sitting in the clubhouse I overhead a touch of dry Finnish humour. Someone was asked how they had got on and the answer came back: "Not very good, we had trouble in Sweden."

Only one more round to go, but it

SUNSET OR SUNRISE?
Actually, it's both. It's 2.45am and already the sun is rising.

occurred to me that I had barely seen most of the other competitors who were either out on the course or probably in bed. It was quite a lonely battle especially at night when the rest of Tornio and its twin city of Haparanda were sensibly asleep and there was a dankness in the air and an eerie mist hovering over the fairways.

That afternoon we headed for the unbelievable heat of a savu sauna, which literally means smoke sauna. It was an attempt to de-knot the muscles that were tightening with every shot. A savu sauna is a remarkable concept. A huge pile of boulders, each the size of a watermelon, sit in a corner of an outbuilding with a fire beneath them. It takes around eight hours to 'warm' up but then you have a radiant heat of incredible dryness and intensity. The blackened room is a calming if smoky place to be, but relaxes you quicker than valium. You can potter in and out and dive in the nearby stream for several hours if you like, because the stones can keep their heat until morning. But we had to go for a slice of reindeer and berry sauce and a few medicinal beers – remember the mozzies – before our final

push at half past midnight.

When we set off with the laugh-a-minute pair of Paul and Jorma, the sun was out there somewhere but it was shrouded in deep, menacing clouds, and fingers of lightning were reaching for the pine tops. Dew clung to every blade of grass and the waters were ghostly still. It was totally quiet except for our friendly banter, and the grumbling thunder slowly disappearing towards Sweden. But it was around Amen Corner again that I experienced another once-in-a-lifetime phenomena. Looking down the 11th fairway was a magical sight. The storm had cleared and a haze hung limply on the silver birches and dragged itself across the fairway, as the sun was on its way up from its nadir, its orange glow tickling the treetops. Wow! It was just before three in the morning and I was witnessing a life-enhancing moment.

It was to get better. As our last few holes came into sight, everywhere was bathed in a glorious golden light. It was an atmosphere of deep calm and the glow made you glad to be alive. A birdie to sign off with made me glance back across the reedy waters and take

a mental photograph to capture what had turned out to be a wonderful adventure. I had quite forgotten the time, and the post-round beers seemed natural and more poignant now that I had seen the real Lapland Gold. It was 5.15 in the morning and I had 90 holes under my belt, and memories to savour.

When after three rounds I had felt it was all becoming a bit of a chore and was questioning my powers to get excited, I was now bathing in an extraordinary feeling of well-being which made all the lack of sleep worthwhile. Our team was hopelessly adrift of the winners, but that's not what it was all about. I had done something unusual, something that could be locked away in my golfing memory banks forever.

We spent the afternoon rafting down the Tornio river and generally loafing about before the prize-giving barbecue. Veikko and his merry band had been victorious but he was the only one there to collect his colour TV. Rude? No, not at all. The other five had all made their apologies. Where were they? In bed? No, they were out on the course playing in another 54-hole non-stop marathon. Hullu, bloody Hullu!

WAY PAST BEDTIME
11-year-old Little Miss Linda Henriksson has aleady won a longest drive competition.

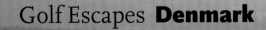

Björn leaves his mark

Western Denmark not only features some of the best natural heathland courses outside Britain, it's where a young Thomas Björn cut his golfing teeth. Golf World makes the short hop across the North Sea for a three-day break in Jutland.

Words: **Gary Firkins**   Photography: **Bob Atkins**

onjure up, if you would, an image of your favourite heathland golf course – Wentworth, Sunningdale, Ganton, or perhaps Gleneagles. Think of those firm, tightly-cropped fairways and fast-running greens bordered by heather, birch, bracken and pine.

Now imagine flying over the sea to Continental Europe and a land that emerges out of the blue as a great wall of white sand and heaving dune, but which rapidly gives way to acre upon acre of wild, rolling heath, punctuated by the odd farmstead and hamlet.

This is Jutland, the great finger of western Denmark pointing into the North Sea. And as far as landscapes go, there can't be many more naturally suited to golf.

In Britain, it's no coincidence that when golf's founding fathers turned their backs on the sea in search of inland terrain on which to build courses they fell upon sandy, links-like patches of heathland. And that's why, even though Jutland is a foreign land and golf is a

Forget the wine with dinner, Danes prefer their beers.

Denmark or Berkshire? The heathland terrain around Silkeborg makes for the perfect natural golf course.

relatively recent import, the golfer feels instinctively at home here.

The soil is admittedly softer and more peaty than anything one would find underfoot in Surrey or Berkshire, but the outstanding feature of golf in this part of Denmark is its closeness to nature. The senses come alive to the sights, sounds and smells of a country that is free from overcrowding and the polluting effects of cars and planes. And even though golf only took off here in the 1960s and 1970s, there are already many quality courses.

Silkeborg's 170-yard 6th hole was designed by the club's most famous member – Thomas Björn.

"The 4th on the Blue Course is a 369m (404-yard) par-4 that plunges

It's a long haul up and down the hills of Vejle's tree-lined course.

Probably the most extraordinary par-4 in Europe: the 404-yard 4th at Vejle plunges into a tree-lined valley.

Holiday homes and wooden shacks nestle in the dunes north of Holstebro. Jutland is blessed with vast beaches.

Holstebro is ranked 96th in Golf World's Top 100 of Continental Courses; Vejle winds impressively through towering beech woods; and Silkeborg, with its long, tricky, tree-lined holes, is where Thomas Björn learnt his powerful but precise game. And it's at Silkeborg, in the heart of the Danish lake district, that I start my three-day break.

Although the club was founded in 1966, Silkeborg is one of Denmark's more established clubs and its course is considered to be among the top five in the country. The clubhouse may be in the slightly stark, modern Scandinavian style, but the feel of the place is traditional.

One topic of conversation dominates the bar – Thomas Björn. As a junior member who went on to become the first Dane to play in the Ryder Cup, Thomas is the club's favourite son. His clubs and bag from Valderrama '97 form a shrine in a corner of the clubhouse.

from a tee in high heaven to the very depths of the underworld."

THE COURSES

Silkeborg

Length: 6,159m (6,735 yards).
Par: 71.
Hilly heathland course with excellent variety of challenging tree-lined holes. Look out for some superb elevated tees.
Call: 0045 86853399.

Holstebro

Length: 6,233m (6,816 yards).
Par: 72.
Pure heathland terrain with some classic holes. Lots of tactical, dog-legged par-4s and outstanding par-3s. It could be Sunningdale.
Call: 0045 97485155.

Vejle

Length: 5,791m (6,333 yards).
Par: 72.
Woodland and parkland course that features the most extraordinary par-4 in Europe. Too quirky to be a top-quality course but good fun nevertheless.
Call: 0045 75858185.

Club manager Niels Jørgen Steenbjerg remembers the young Björn taking up the game as a seven year old. "As we would say, he got it from his mother's milk," he laughs. "Both his parents were keen golfers and his older brother, Søren, was a good player too.

"Of course, Thomas was very competitive when he was young. Even then he had a great temper, but he's better at controlling it now."

Out on the course, the fairways wend their way through heather and pine trees and first impressions are that you really could be at Sunningdale rather than Silkeborg. The most impressive physical feature of this terrain is a high ridge of sand hills that heave the course skywards. Like a giant ramp the holes run up, down and across this range. The result is uphill holes that require precise iron approaches together with some

Jutland's towns are small and quiet. Here in Holstebro the local attractions are, how should we say it, limited.

spectacular plunging drives from elevated tees. The 17th, a monstrous 493m (540-yard) par-5, sweeps away through the trees like a downhill skiing course.

Standing on this tee as a milky evening sun sets into the mist and tree tops, the full sense of peace and quiet in this part of the world hits home. Only the sound of birds heralding twilight can be heard. That and the occasional 'bink' of my titanium driver.

Unlike Zealand, Denmark's easternmost island and home to cosmopolitan Copenhagen, Jutland is quiet and sparsely populated. Sleepy villages are connected by roads that have little traffic. Even towns like Silkeborg seem to have little going on and there is no nightlife to speak of, except for Saturdays. But if you are content playing golf by day and enjoying homely food

The village church at Husby. Place-names here and in eastern England share a common Viking heritage.

Spectacular views over the beech woods from the Munkebjerg Hotel.

and good beer in a quiet restaurant by night, then you'll like Jutland. Whatever, the Danes are extremely welcoming.

On my way to Holstebro, little more than an hour's drive from Silkeborg, I stop off at an intriguing little church at Husby. From nowhere a friendly villager, Tage Meller, appears and shows me round the 12th century building. I mention than many village names I've seen on roadsigns en route seem familiar. That, of course, is thanks to the Vikings who not only gave names to the villages of their homeland but brought their words to settlements in eastern and northern England. Place-names like Kirkby, Lowestoft, Scunthorpe and Braithwaite are wholly Old Danish. In the case of Kirkby, a common village name in the English Midlands (meaning village with a church) and Husby in Jutland (meaning village with houses), it's easy to see the similarities and how the names were formed.

Holstebro Golf Club is among the best three courses in Denmark. It is an outstanding layout that is as pure a test of heathland golf as any in Britain even though it is only 30 years old. It's strength lies in its use of natural features. Instead of fairway bunkers, great heathery knolls reach out into the fairway to form chicanes around and through which the golfer must thread his drives. On top of this, many of the par-4s are

Visit website: www.golftravelclub.com
Where to stay: Hotel Schaumberg in Holstebro; Hotel Louisiana in Silkeborg and Hotel Munkebjerg in Vejle are all four-star hotels close to the courses and can be booked through the Golf Travel Club.
When to go: Summer is slightly shorter in Scandinavia, but can be drier than the UK.

May to September are the best months for golf. Courses can be busy at the weekends, but reservations on weekdays are rarely necessary.
Tourist offices: The Danish Tourist Board in London can be contacted at: 55 Sloane Street, London, SW1X 9SY; tel 020 7259 5959 (open Monday to Friday 10am-3pm).

"You'll find Bill Rogers' winning sweater from the 1981 Open"

The Golf Museum downstairs at the Munkejberg Hotel.

doglegs where views of the green are obscured from the tee so there's a premium on placing drives precisely.

The best hole is the 494m (540-yard) par-5 2nd. It plays through a corridor of trees and heather that seem to reach out and grab your ball at any opportunity.

This is a class golf course and is remarkable value for money. The only disappointment is the clubhouse which is as drab as a dilapidated primary school. But after experiencing a course of this quality, it's hard to be upset.

If you have time, it's well worth taking a short drive from Holstebro out to the coast. Jutland is blessed with vast beaches and mountainous dunelands. Had golf arrived earlier in this country, before the time of environmental legislation, there probably would be many links courses – and good ones too judging by the scale of the dunes.

Scattered among the sand hills are wooden shacks; holiday homes for some; full time residences for others. I stop off

for a beer in one of the beachside cafés just as a shower scuds in off the North Sea and salts the windows.

On the other side of Jutland, on the eastern coast, and about an hour and a half drive, lies Vejle. Unlike the heathland courses of Silkeborg and Holstebro, Vejle Golf Club is set amid majestic, mature beech woods. Here you will find possibly the most amazing golf hole in Europe.

The 4th on the Blue Course (there are three loops of nine) is a 369m (404-yard) par-4 that plunges from a tee in high heaven to the very depths of the underworld. And with the fairway bottle-necking and then dog-legging to the right, with water down both sides, it's an horrendously difficult tee shot.

My 4-iron (okay, so I'm chickening out) launches high above the tree tops and then falls, and falls, and falls. And then falls some more before finally finding the fairway. Whether it's a good hole or not, it's certainly the most exhilarating of par-4s.

The rest of the course is a mixture of parkland and woodland. It's the holes through the cathedral-high beech trees that really catch the eye, though. Some are impossibly tight, especially when a solitary beech has been left in the middle of the fairway.

Because of its quirks, Vejle is not quite up to the same standard as Holstebro and Silkeborg, but it's still fun to play.

Next door to the course is the Munkebjerg Hotel which boasts what was the first golf museum on Continental Europe. Here you will find, among other oddments of golfing memorabilia, Bill Rogers' winning sweater from the 1981 Open and Gene Sarazen's plus-fours.

Jutland may not be an obvious golfing destination, but with the quality of courses and their value for money it's certainly worth the hop east. And if you get bored with all that wild healthland, duneland and woodland, there's always the plastic alternative next to the airport on the way home – Legoland.

STILL PLAYING THE WHITE MAN'S GAME

WHAT IT'S REALLY LIKE: TO PLAY GOLF IN SOUTH AFRICA

Leopard Rock Golf Club, Zimbabwe. Challenging golf with unbelievable views.

With the rand worth only slightly more than a peanut, touring golfers in South Africa can live like lords. As long as they are white and middle aged, it seems.

Words: **Steve Carr** Main photograph: **Allsport**

"Here is your caddie, sir, his name is Molatwane, you can call him Bushy."

A dishevelled 20-something siddled up and we shook hands. It wasn't the strength of his grip or his comically sporadic facial hair that stood out most, it was his other arm, which was bloodily bandaged from his elbow to his fingertips. "What happened to you?" I asked naively, "I had a knife fight over my wife last night with a man who wanted her for his own. He's taken her." I stood shocked, wondering at the insignificance of hiring a bag carrier who, with much more important things on his mind, and severely injured, had nevertheless turned up for work. South Africa is a land of contrasts for sure, both good and bad, and as a travelling golfer you will see much of it, warthogs and all.

Sense may have prevailed and the black vote now counts, but you can't pretend that all is colourful harmony like the Republic's nickname – The Rainbow Nation – suggests. But it is getting there. Once the name may have stood for racism, anarchy, injustice, you get my Rorke's (drift that is). It is now more

Above: The greenkeeping staff at Selbourne Country Club on the KwaZulu-Natal coast. In fact, this picture could have been taken almost anywhere in South Africa.

Right: Erinvale: You can expect a quality golf course with some spectacular mountain views.

ANGUS MURRAY

BOB ATKINS

likely to mean rejuvenation, adventure and intoxicating.

Any divide that exists still, and it does despite who is in power, is noticeable in golf. Whether anyone likes it or not, golf is still a white man's preserve. President Thabo Mbeki may have been made Honorary Chairman of the President's Cup in 2003 to be held at Fancourt, but he knows more about leg-irons than he does 5-irons.

But before getting caught up in the social injustice debate, do not lose sight of the fact that if you are a golfer, then this diverse country gives you incredible opportunities to add to your golfing experiences and education. There are now over 450 courses in this vast land, and just like the people, they are a mix of 'cultures'.

You can walk into a humble country course along with pick-up driving farmers, where the clubhouse is a modest, unedifying affair, the greens khaki and the ball bounds like a springbok on the hard-baked earth. Or you can swan through whitewashed gates to a glass and steel palace overlooking a Garden of Eden landscape. Links or heath, bushveld or parkland, golf can be a wonderful adventure beneath the biggest skies on earth.

If you are white, aged between 35 and 60 then you will fit in nicely. If you are black, then you're more likely to be tending the greens or carrying bags. There is no dispute on this. In Sun City recently, the famed resort that acts out its fantasies in the bowl of an extinct volcano north west of Johannesburg, an amusing, if not surprising, scene was all around us. At the Gary Player Country Club, home of the Million Dollar Challenge, each and every fourball consisted of a quartet of white men, of the ages described, in a close to identical uniform. Almost without fail each one wore a pair of safari brown shorts, a predominantly white polo shirt and a baseball cap. With each group four black caddies in matching green overalls lolloped along behind. In the pleasant clubhouse, more of the same existed, except 'the boys' had swapped their caps for a chilled beer, mobile phones and talk of cricket and rugby, and the waiters were now black. It gave a whole new meaning to the phrase 'Golf Boers'.

Golf here is very much still for the executive white crowd but maybe there is some change on the horizon. Omar Sandys, a black African now plying his trade on Tour, is a hot prospect especially since he has some heavyweight backing

from Darren Clarke and Lee Westwood. I have also played with a black 1-handicapper near Cape Town. But they are a rarity. Soweto too, the township of four million outside Johannesburg, has a course of sorts enthusiastically run by the locals. It is about the only one in South Africa where rarely you will find a white man treading the fairways. But mainly the only coloureds are to be found in the fly-ridden caddie shacks or pulling up weeds.

Even here they get a rough ride. You cannot walk into a locker room without seeing a notice about the propensity of your bagman to be dishonest. 'Keep your valuables about your person not in your golf bag.' Talk about tarring everyone with the same brush. You are told also not to tip your caddie too much, even though to the exchange-rate-happy tourist, 'too much' might be small beer. Apparently once overtipped, it can become always expected, and also jealousy prevails.

If you are not comfortable with having a caddie and playing the white middle-aged thing, then golf in South Africa may not be for you. But I would urge you to go with the flow. You will have a fantastic time. Who in their right mind would give up the opportunity to play under

"If you are white, aged between 35 and 60, then you will fit in nicely. If you are black, then you're more likely to be tending the greens or carrying golf bags"

Leopard Creek Golf Club: Avoid the bunkers and you'll have a chance of recording a good score.

heat heavy skies with a bagman at your side, often a real character, for about £5 a round, if also you know that you are helping to feed a family along the way? It is a fact of life here.

Yes the socially conscious of us may feel initially awkward, but you don't hear too many of the caddies complaining either. To most, carrying a bag is decently paid relief from the hardships of either unemployment or manual labour.

The way the caddie shacks are run differs with the territory. Go to one of the clubs of repute and mostly you will see well-groomed and uniformed bagmen marshalled by a jovial caddie master. The locals and members often have an arrangement with a regular and pre-book their man. Go down market somewhat and the caddying doesn't do any favours to those that suggest it is an art. Here it is more a survival of the fittest. The only 'uniform' is to have a pair of shoes that have more soul than sole.

But wherever you go don't be surprised if the caddies are wincing at your every slash into the scrub, chuckling at your birdies and generally chuntering

excitedly in Zulu or Shona among themselves – they inevitably will have a side bet going on you. It took a few rounds to twig, until once I spotted a disconsolate boy sloping off the 18th and another whooping with delight at a final hole birdie, his lunch money doubled. Talk about pressure – playing for someone else's food.

That same diversity of character is echoed in the courses themselves. Royal Cape was Africa's first course built in the late 1800s and as the popularity has grown among natives and tourists, the style of club has also evolved. Today courses are being built by major names. Jack Nicklaus has just opened up his first in the continent at Pecanwood, an hour north of Jo'burg. Tom Weiskopf has created a modern thoroughbred bumbling down to the Indian Ocean at Zimbali near Durban, while Gary Player still rules the roost.

Once there were just members' courses for expats and colonialists. Now entire resorts have been created for the second homers and the almost six million visitors that come to South Africa each year to feel the excitement of an emerging

nation.

Genuine world class courses may just keep the fingers of one hand occupied (probably the Montagu course at Fancourt, Durban Country Club and the Gary Player CC), but there are so many fabulous second stringers that any hardened golf traveller would still go home more than happy.

Most European tourists glide into The Cape to start, and it is truly one of the world's greatest destinations with the Mother City of Cape Town as its focus. It may not be the heartbeat of Africa that more adventurous souls crave but, because it is the most cosmopolitan region of the country, it is perhaps where the rainbow gleams brightest.

But for all its wonderment, fun and high living, the golf is not breathtaking. Royal Cape has the history and the ambience of class, but is very good rather than great. The city courses like Mowbray and Rondesbosch might have Table Mountain as a backdrop and are perfectly decent but they are uninspiring to those seeking real golfing thrills.

But it is strange. Golf in these parts and up into Stellenbosch and down to

FANCOURT: Regarded as South Africa's classiest golf resort.

BOB ATKINS

Somerset West and Erinvale, has a quality that is not necessarily linked to the majesty of the courses. Somehow there is a feel good factor that transcends the links. Perhaps it is just that life in these parts is pretty ruddy good for we swallows. Perhaps it is that we feel more at home here than anywhere else in Africa. Perhaps it is just the wine.

For more serious and head swimming golf, head east along the Garden Route. Take in Arabella near Hermanus, and the three stunning courses at Fancourt in George under the gaze of the Outeniqua Mountains. Further north, at Hans Merensky and Malalane next door to the Kruger National Park, you'll probably see young bucks and warthogs, giraffe, hippos and crocs. Crocodiles are a little surprise up at the Lost City course at Sun City. A purpose built pool on the 13th is crawling with the scaly creatures. Real Africa no, but memorable theatre.

South Africa has an allure that can both calm and perturb. When you stand on the Indian Ocean coast among the fynbos and dunes where the crickets rattle out their monotonous tune you have a sense of space. Look north and behind you is the blue yonder – next stop Antarctica. In front, thousands of miles of heat and dust, forest and plain, and a bewildering array of cultures and even anguish and degradation.

On the courses of this remarkable country rarely do you feel so imbued with the spirit of enterprise, but at the same time so privileged. It's inspiring to play for fun under agitated clouds where the mother of all storms may be brewing that'll have the wildlife scampering for cover. But I also revel in the fact that you can experience opulence for sweet SA. The rand, so long the currency synonymous with gold and diamonds, is worth peanuts to world travellers. At over 17 rand to the pound, double what it was a year ago, everything including golf is unbelievable value. Green fees can range from around R50 up to the rare levels of R300 (£2.50-£15). And anyhow, the halfway house Castle lager and a boerwoers sausage for around a quid are pretty good too.

South Africa's golfing culture may mean you see more middle England couples, and large hairy men with khaki shorts and moustaches than might be healthy, but put away your PC hat for a moment. This country is a world to be discovered, to be cherished but above all respected for what it is – a ripe, changing nation.

THE GOLFING HOTSPOTS

NORTH WEST PROVINCE
Sun City
■ 2 hours NW of Johannesburg.
Two courses rumble their way through the bush at this theatrical resort. The best known Gary Player CC is 7,700 yards of the back tees! But do not despair, since you are playing at a heady 6,000 feet above sea level. The Lost City course is even more surreal built in a desert style, but both are in fantastic condition.
Contacts:
Tel: 0027 14 557 1245.
Fax: 0027 14 557 3902.
email: sshearer@sunint.co.za www.sun-international.com

KWAZULU NATAL
Durban Country Club
■ 10 minutes north of city.
This is the only course in the continent of Africa that is rated in the world's Top 100 at 89th – with good reason. It is a wild challenge, set through undulating scrub and dunes close to the ocean. Breathtaking and fearsome in the wind.
Contacts:
Tel: 0027 31 3131777.
Fax: 0027 31 31700.
email: sandera@dcclub.co.za www.dcclub.co.za

NORTHERN PROVINCE
Hans Merensky
■ On the edge of Kruger National Park at Phalaborwa. A real African adventure. You are likely to see buffalo, giraffe and the odd leopard if you're lucky while crocs and hippos lurk around the low, wooden river bridge at the 17th.
Contacts:
Tel: 0027 15 7813931.
Fax: 0027 15 781 5309.
email: elaine@hansmerensky.com www.hansmerensky.com

WESTERN CAPE
Fancourt
■ 4 hours east of Cape Town in George.
Your only dilemma is which of the four sparkling courses to choose. The Montagu is the finest and a soothing ride among the bush and flirting lakes, but the Links will hold the Presidents Cup in 2003. South Africa's classiest golf resort.
Contacts:
Tel: 0027 44 804 0000.
Fax: 0027 44 804 0700.
email: hotel@fancourt.co.za www.fancourt.co.za

CAPE TOWN
Milnerton
■ 15 minutes north of the city centre. Play this renovated links more for its position than the quality of the golf. Though very good, Milnerton has incredible views back along the beach towards Table Mountain and the city, and out to sea towards Robben Island, prison for Nelson Mandela for over 20 years.
Contact:
Tel: 0027 21 552 1047.
Fax: 0027 21 551 5987.
email: milgolf@intekom.co.za

BOB ATKINS

Desert •
Classic

Voted Emerging Golf Destination of the Year, Dubai has much to offer the visiting golfer. Those looking for a unique and rigorous challenge will find what they're looking for in the middle of a desert.

Words: **Anne Harper**

We boldly drove along the inside lip of the towering red sand dune, like surfers riding a gigantic frozen wave. Our young Arab driver, clad in his traditional white robes, didn't appear to have a nerve in his body as the tyres of the four-wheel-drive jeep stalled momentarily, spewing great clouds of rusty dust into the air, before plummeting down yet another dune. With stomachs still somewhere near the upper reaches of the ceiling, the convoy of vehicles on this sand safari wove across the endless desert, halting at an Arabic camp. In the gathering dusk we enjoyed displays of falconry, pipe smoking and belly dancing – the latter with plenty of audience participation. Around us gathered the silent desert and salt flats stretching eastward towards the mountains while, above, the inky blackness of the night sky danced with millions upon millions of stars.

"You should have seen this place 20 years ago," recalled one of our party, as we sipped mint tea around a flickering camp-fire. "The creek was a squalid waterway and we crossed it in a shabby and quite dangerous little boat. Everywhere there was construction work going on, and all you could see off the coastline in the Gulf was an endless queue of merchant ships laden with bricks, timber and steel just waiting to berth with materials to build the place."

A generation ago Dubai was a humble Bedouin society. Today it is one of the most dazzling cities on earth. A fabulous 21st century oasis, created by the visionary Maktoum ruling family from their oil riches, has risen out of the endless desert to become one of the most liberal and dynamic Arab states. It is also becoming the first holiday choice of an increasing number of golfers, and in 2001 was voted Emerging Golf Destination of the Year by the International Association of Golf Tour Operators.

The key event, which has propelled Dubai onto the world golfing stage, is the annual Dubai Desert Classic, a prestigious date on the European Tour calendar, attracting the cream of the world's golfers. Past champions include Fred Couples, José Maria Olazábal,

"Everything about Dubai attracts a superlative. Its boulevards are handsome, its skyscrapers dramatic. The city positively bursts with the best of everything"

Colin Montgomerie, Ernie Els and Seve Ballesteros.

It began in 1989, just a year after the Emirates Golf Club threw open its doors to reveal The Majilis, the first grass golf course in the Middle East and one clearly designed for championships with a 7,101-yard layout over rolling desert terrain. The course includes huge sand waste bunkers, adding to the desert feel, and one of the most dramatic finishing holes to be found anywhere, with players negotiating a long dogleg and a lake. When Ballesteros played here in this year's Dubai Desert Classic he told the BBC that he believed it to be the "best course in the world".

There's barely a free room in the city when the Desert Classic rolls in to town, particularly as it is accompanied by the Dubai Shopping Festival, preceded by the $1 million Dubai Tennis Open and followed by the richest horse race on the planet, the Dubai World Cup.

However, with a prize list of over £1 million, the Dubai Desert Classic doesn't exactly struggle for top class entries and Els warmed up for his nail-biting Open success in July by becoming the first double winner of the tournament.

Majilis was followed by a second course, the Wadi in 1996. Wadi is dominated by a landscaped river, and both courses enjoy the facilities of a spectacular clubhouse, designed to resemble a tented Bedouin village.

Both Danish European Tour player Thomas Bjorn and his British born golf coach Pete Cowen are based here each winter, taking advantage of the superb climate to practise away from the inclement weather of Northern Europe.

By the time the Wadi course opened, Dubai had already added two more impressive courses to its golf portfolio. In 1993 the Dubai Creek Golf and Yacht Club was opened, its 18-hole championship course poised dramatically alongside the creek, and its clubhouse, designed to resemble an Arab sailing boat, is now one of Dubai's great landmarks.

The course itself has some tricky doglegs and features three ornamental lakes and other seawater hazards. However, the creek itself is the most memorable hazard of all, running alongside the 17th and 18th holes to guarantee every player an exciting finale.

In the same year that Dubai Creek was opened, a linksy style nine-hole course was created inside the perimeter of the racecourse at Nad Al Sheba to create the Dubai Golf and Racing Club. Three years later another nine were added, running alongside the home straight and the entire course was floodlit.

Golf under floodlights is an experience everyone should try. The night-time novice will need to develop new etiquette skills on the greens where floodlights illuminate the turf from all points of the compass. Eyes in the back of your head are a definite advantage as you strive to avoid casting one of your multiple shadows over a playing partner's line.

An excellent nine-hole grass course is available at the Jebel Ali hotel. This super layout, running alongside a picturesque marina, features a salt lake, which comes into play on five of the holes. I was one of 2,000 guests enjoying the Jebel Ali Challenge match the day before the Dubai Classic teed off. There was alfresco dining and the chance to watch six of the world's top players play in a charity match, which has become an annual must-do diary date in Dubai. The

real joy of it was watching Thomas Bjorn paired with Colin Montgomerie, successfully defending their title against the pairings of Darren Clarke and Padraig Harrington and Ernie Els with Mark O'Meara.

Monty has had a big hand in seeing a further chapter written in the golfing book of Dubai with the opening of Montgomerie Dubai course in 200 acres at the Emirates Hills, part of a luxury residential development. He is one of the design partners in the project, which features a superb golf academy and a challenging layout, designed to host a future Dubai Classic. Work is also under way on a second course being built here by Monty's co-architect, Desmond Muirhead, and this time his golf legend partner is Greg Norman.

It takes millions of gallons of water to keep all these fairways in top condition and each course is supported by desalination plants pumping water in from the Gulf, linked to state of the art, computer controlled irrigation systems. This is why the green fees are on the high side. The Nad al Sheba starts at around £43 for a round while the new Montgomerie Dubai will cost around £100, and there are strict handicap limits of 28 for men and 36 for ladies at all the Dubai courses, while soft spikes are a must.

If, at the end of the day, you cannot resist the call of the desert, the Dubai Country Club, the oldest golf club in Dubai, offers a different golfing experience playing from sand or "brown" courses. Golfers carry a small piece of artificial turf with them and use it to play with off the fairways. Further out in the mountains at the Hatta Fort Hotel there is a rather fun 1,057 yards cross-country

When playing golf in
the desert expect
plenty of sand traps.

THE WEATHER

Dubai's is a sun worshipper's dream between October and April ranging from 25 to 35 degrees. High humidity and 37-41 degrees in the summer should see off most Europeans.

golf course with artificial greens and tees and the rest is just, well "brown".

Dubai is a wonderful place to enjoy a holiday, not only because of its excellent golf, but also because there is plenty to keep a non-golfing partner happy too. You could enjoy a holiday in one of the

shopping malls alone.

Dubai is a tropical beach resort with a dazzling skyscraper skyline. It offers a safe, welcoming environment with beautiful parks, magnificent sports facilities and shops equal to anything on offer at Fifth Avenue or Bond Street.

Take dinner on an Arab yacht, gracefully cruising the creek or hop aboard a water taxi to the bustle of the ancient gold and spice stores. Enjoy horse or camel racing and try a sand safari in the stunning desert.

Everything about Dubai attracts a

An oasis in the desert ...that's the Dubai Creek Golf Club.

"We have some of the best courses in the world. But Dubai has a lot more than just golf – wonderful beaches, watersports, hotels, and the magic of the desert"

superlative. Its boulevards are handsome, its skyscrapers dramatic. The shops are luxuriously awash with designer goods and haggling is part of the shopping experience. The city positively bursts with the best of everything and this can be seen in the quite uncanny way that it just does not seem to possess a poor hotel.

Some of their best hotels have even become stars in their own right. Such as the impossibly luxurious six-star Burj al Arab with its gold leaf pillars and Star Wars lobby. Another landmark is the oft-photographed Jumeriah Beach – shaped like a huge wave. The architecture of the recently opened Emirates Tower hotel with its companion office block is simply breathtaking. The solitude and understated luxury of The Jumeriah Beach Club was much appreciated by the England football team and their families for a pre-World Cup break.

Even though Dubai enjoys a liberal lifestyle, it still has strict no alcohol laws –

the drink licenses have been awarded to the hotels, making them the focus of the city's social scene and this is where you will find top class restaurants and nightclubs. The Jumeriah Beach alone has 12 restaurants offering every type of cuisine imaginable, including a little fish and seafood restaurant at the end of a pier.

Still it grows. Everywhere you can see and hear the rattle of frantic construction work. One of the most notable projects must be Palm Islands – two identical man-made palm islands being created out into the Arabian Gulf complete with boutique hotels, exclusive villas, shopping and entertainment. The Dubai Marina is the first residential development offering expatriates the chance to own property and 2004 will see the opening of the Dubai Festival City featuring a 55-storey tower, amphitheatre, restaurants, shops, hotels, cinemas and apartments.

Rod Bogg, the energetic and passionate

managing director of the Emirates Golf Club, has been in Dubai from the start of its golf development and has witnessed the city and Emirate's rapid transformation into a world-class holiday and business destination.

On receiving the award for Emerging Destination of 2001, Rod said: "We have fabulous golfing facilities in Dubai. We have some of the best courses in the world and without doubt some of the best clubhouses. But Dubai has a lot more than just golf – wonderful beaches, water sports, the best hotels, not forgetting the magic of the desert."

When I caught up with him at the Dubai Desert Classic in March he was still bustling with pride at the Emerging Golf Destination award, but in typical fashion he had one eye on the future: "We've got that now. We've emerged. We're now looking ahead."

And you'd better believe him, because Dubai has definitely got what it takes.

The pyramid game

It's the world capital of history and stuffed with atmosphere, but what does Egypt offer for the holiday golfer? Peter Masters reveals all.

Photography: **James Cheadle**

Gary Player has sown the seeds of
Egyptian golf at Cascades —
easily the country's finest course.

Not a giant tee marker, a pyramid. They out number golf courses by eight to one.

A traffic jam, Egyptian-style. Bringing the harvest from the banks of the Nile.

Y ou can hardly hear the engines. JUST a low rhythmic thud as the boat heads out into mid-stream, where the orange of the evening sun catches the tips of the waves and bursts into flames. Around a bend in the river a town appears, a mixture of ancient temples and colonial hotels clustered along the eastern bank. It looks as if the buildings are dipping their toes into the water.

Luxor is busy tonight. Its inhabitants are milling about, embarking on 'Death on the Nile' cruises, sipping cocktails on riverside balconies, and jumping into small, single-sailed boats known as

The world's longest river, the Nile is also the lifeblood of Egypt and its people.

feluccas. Voices come drifting across the water, their provenance unclear. Snapshots of laughter catch on the breeze before dying away in the night air.

This is a moment of pure serenity in the heart of Egypt – in the heart of the Nile, a river whose gentle flow has given life to a civilisation 2,000 years older than Christ. Over the port bow the sun is falling towards the serrated edge of the desert mountains, where the tombs of Tutankhamen and Ramses II are secreted within the Valley of the Kings. To our left stand the great statues of ancient pharaohs and the pillars of the Temple of Luxor. On this boat, on this night, the magical appeal of Egypt is all laid out before us – thousands of chapters of history.

Our own exploration here is hardly Dr Livingstone and his quest for the Nile – we are hunting for great golf under the Saharan sun. Nonetheless, it has unearthed some unexpected gems. Names like Katameya Heights, the Cascades, Mirage City – and, of course, Ronan from Tralee. Ronan Gillooly is the club pro at Royal Valley Golf Club near Luxor, and his presence on our riverboat provides the golfing flavour.

He is a small man whose brown, leathery complexion suggests he has spent most of his years outdoors – and probably not in Tralee. His accent is unmistakably Emerald Isle, though, and

An Egyptian family at home on the farm.

Here's looking at you kid!

Jewels on the Nile

With names like Mirage City, Dreamland and Royal Valley, Egyptian courses promise big. But do they deliver? Here is our verdict on six of the best.

Katameya Heights

New Cairo City, Cairo.
6,780 yards, par 72
Designer: Yves Bureau.
Character: This club oozes quality from the moment you climb the drive to the palatial clubhouse, with its bird's eye view of the estate. The course is hilly and surrounded by wealthy homes, but strangely this enhances its appeal. There is a stadium feel to many holes, and the conditioning of the course is faultless.
Signature hole: The 15th, from a panoramic tee, is one to remember. It's a par-5 with water on the left, where the drive is all important.
Call: 0020 27 580512.

Mirage City

New Cairo City, Cairo.
6,985 yards, par 72
Designer: Peter Harridine.
Character: This is a plush resort course in front of Marriott's new Mirage City Hotel complex, which opens next year and will boast the biggest spa in the world. The layout is less hilly than at nearby Katameya Heights, especially on the front nine, but there is much more water to contend with here.
Signature hole: Two spring to mind. The 5th, a short, cute par-4 with an approach over water; and the 12th, a picturesque par-3.
Call: 0020 24 085200.

Dreamland

Sixth of October Road, Cairo.
7,205 yards, par 72
Designer: Karl Litten.
Character: We played here in a sand storm, which could easily have spoiled the experience were it not for the obvious quality of the course. As a championship test for the skilled golfer, this has the edge on the resort offerings nearby. Litten is an expert in the desert, having created the Emirates Course at Dubai.
Signature hole: Tough rather than spectacular, Dreamland's best holes are tight, testing par-5s. They are the second and sixth holes on each nine.
Call: 0020 11 400577.

Royal Valley

near Luxor.
6,735 yards, par 72
Designer: Arthur Davis.
Character: Although relatively flat, this is a course that will keep your interest from start to finish thanks to its intelligent use of bunkering and sandy waste areas. A terrifically balanced test – which makes it ideal for those planning to visit several times in a week.
Signature hole: A large reservoir is sandwiched between the 10th and 18th holes, both par-5s. No matter how steely your nerve, these two are challenging.
Call: 0020 12 2129204.

Cascades

Soma Bay, Red Sea.
6,864 yards, par 72
Designer: Gary Player.
Character: The best course in Egypt. Laid out over the bleak desert sands, every hole has a very individual appeal, so that you feel you could roll each one up and move it somewhere else. What it lacks in collective character it makes up for in the thrill of the design.
Signature hole: The par-3 5th, with a green that bites into the Red Sea, is the obvious candidate, but the double fairway on the 12th makes it one for the strategy buffs.
Call: 0020 65 544901.

Steigenberger

El Gouna, Red Sea.
6,775 yards, par 72
Designer: Gene Bates/Fred Couples.
Character: Many Germans holiday here, as the name suggests, and the overall quality of the resort is top-notch. The golf course is not the most demanding you'll find, and that might come as a relief after you've warmed up on the spectacular practice ground, where you hit shots of varying lengths to a number of island greens.
Signature hole: For braver players, the direct line to the par-4 15th will be rewarded if you can avoid both water and sand.
Call: 0020 10 1551015.

in the company of fellow westerners on a boat with a free bar, he is in jocular mood.

"What I've really been missing is good conversation," Ronan says as he scours the beer selection for the giveaway black and gold can. "It can get a bit lonely out here sometimes. That's not to say the people are unfriendly, far from it. It's just that they are not like us, if you see what I mean."

"They're Egyptian," I note.

"Exactly. Wonderful aren't they? You know the rich ones sometimes have four wives? Anyway, what did you think of the course – great isn't it? We had a group over from Ireland the other day and they loved it. The weather out here is so wonderful, when golfers start finding out about this place things are really going to take off."

There is a wildness in Ronan's eyes that I put down to enthusiasm mixed with eccentricity. But he is right about his course, right about the weather – apart from the stifling summer, that is – and right about the people too. Waving to the locals from the coach window has been a regular pastime during our trip.

So what about the golf? With 50 million golfers in the world and a travel industry worth $10 billion, Egypt is keen to grab a piece of the action, and our reconnaissance trip will take in three courses in Cairo, three by the Red Sea, and Royal Valley of course. The latter is a good example of how the Egyptians are attempting their seduction of the holiday

"Egypt has 85 pyramids and only ten golf courses. The nine-holer in the shadow of the main pyramid is ideal for photographs."

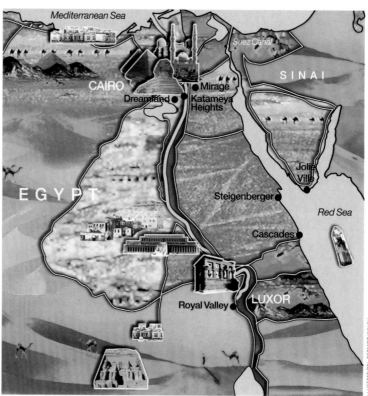

Ornate waterfalls separate the retreating 9th and 18th holes at Cascades.

golf market. Build the course and add the peripherals – the hotels, villas and apartments – later. It is miles from anywhere, and the only approach is by a 20-minute shuttle bus from your hotel in Luxor.

This gives the whole excursion an added excitement, and the ride alone proves an experience. It takes us through Egypt's agricultural outback, where wizened old men with wizened old donkeys sit by the roadside watching the bus go by with expressionless faces. Workers in the fields load wagons with sugar cane beside ramshackle huts made of mud rather than brick – mud stays cooler in the heat. The population of Egypt is similar to the UK's at roughly 60 million, but here everyone lives in a

Our man braves the heat at Dreamland.

corridor along the Nile that occupies just 3.5% of the country.

The golf course itself is encircled by a ten-foot wall – which since there is nothing to keep out, can only be to keep the golfers in. Or perhaps it is something to do with the missile base nearby, which gives a clue to an edgier side of Egyptian life. In 1997 a bomb planted by a militant Islamic group killed more than 60 tourists at Luxor, and you can't set foot out of your hotel without noticing armed guards round every corner. The authorities say there has been no trouble since, but they are taking no chances.

Travelling across the mountains from the Nile to the banks of the Red Sea can only be done at night and with a police escort. The coach travels with all its lights off, and as the mountains loom closer, those of a nervous disposition peer out of the windows and imagine movements in the murky shadows.

In reality there is little or no danger involved, but at a meeting in Cairo with the Minister of Tourism it doesn't take long before the issue gets raised.

Mamdouh El-Beltagui has already admitted his country's naivety when it comes to golf: "We are new into the game," he says. "We still do not know how to reach golfers or how to market the sport, but we are keen to learn."

At which juncture, an American journalist stands up and quizzes him on the security presence and the Middle East problem generally.

"The trouble is at the Gaza Strip, 1,500km away," replies El-Beltagui. "Americans do not know their geography and Gaza can sound like Giza, so it's a linguistic problem."

Since fewer than 15% of Americans possess a passport, our friend decides this is a good time to sit down.

Cairo is dominated by the Giza Plateau, home to three pyramids which have attracted visitors for hundreds of years. From the upper floors of the capital's downtown hotels they can be seen rising above the dusty grey rooftops. Egypt has 85 pyramids in all, but the golf course count has only just moved into double figures. There's a nine-holer in

"Egypt meets the four key criteria – courses, climate, access and value."

the shadows of the main pyramid, Mena House Oberoi, that's ideal for photo opportunities.

The city is polluted, dusty, noisy and busy, yet somehow maintains a mystique. On the road to the Katameya Heights and Mirage City golf courses, for example, we pass the City of the Dead, where market streets and alleys give way to roads that are all but deserted. This is a vast collection of mausoleums, where the only activity is by homeless people, who have no scruples about squatting in a tomb.

"You will see things in Cairo that will amaze and impress you and you'll see things that might shock and disgust you," one hotel official tells us. "There are some fabulous sights and your spending power increases dramatically. But there is animal cruelty. Donkeys get whipped and I've seen horses floating in the Nile."

He proves a wealth of information. The safest bet for food is at the five-star hotels, where business is so profitable that they only need 10% occupancy to break even. You can't, by law, charge a Muslim interest, apparently. And every Egyptian is an entrepreneur.

Which brings us neatly on to 'the Khan', a famous market area which is open every day until midnight. Those familiar with Monty Python's Life of Brian will have an advantage here, because the street bartering is every bit as idiotic as portrayed in the film. You'll get hassled at every stall, and as a general rule should try to settle on a price that is 40% of the one first quoted. For a good deal you must be prepared to stop for a chat. It's a sound idea to mention the man's family, how many children he has – things like that. If you take the trouble to show an interest in him, you'll be amazed how prices can tumble.

While sipping mint tea in one of the quirky alleyways here, we are approached by a boy selling watches. He has them along the length of each arm and in every pocket. He wants 750 Egyptian pounds for a Rolex, but settles in the end for 70 (about £18).

Such experiences are what Egypt is all about. But if you're keen to leave the

THE DETAILS

Plan your trip
How to get there
Several leading airlines offer services from the UK to Cairo. The trip can take between seven and a half and ten hours.

When to go
Average temperatures vary from 57° in January to 90° in summer. Golf can be played throughout the winter, but conditions are ideal in March, April, October and November.

Where to stay
Cairo: Sheraton Tower, call 00202 3369700.
Luxor: Jolie Ville Möven-pick, call 0020 95 374 855.
Soma Bay: Sheraton Soma Bay, call 0020 65 545 845.
El Gouna: Paradisio Beach Hotel, call 0020 65 547 934.
Sharm El-Sheikh: Ritz Carlton, call 0020 69 661 919.

beaten track you might prefer to golf on the southern tip of Sinai, where you'll find Sharm El Sheikh.

Here, breakfast on the sunny patio of the Ritz Carlton finds us discussing our snorkelling adventure of the day before, when dolphins escorted us to a shipwreck, and brightly coloured fish danced on the reef.

This happy image is shattered by the sudden arrival of a bold woman with a complicated hairdo.

"Hi, do you mind if I join you?" she asks, after joining us. I am just about to reply when she turns her attention to a waiter who is trying to deposit a plate of bacon and eggs in front of her.

"I'm a vegetarian," she says with a wave.

Another waiter approaches.

"I don't drink tea or coffee," says Big Hair, gesturing again. The waiters retreat and there is a slight lull before a smartly dressed Egyptian man approaches.

"What can a white girl do to get a drink around here?"

The shock on our faces is unmistakable, but she looks pleased: "Don't worry, he's my husband. I'm Lee from public relations." Lee's hubby flashes a brilliant smile. Her upfront approach has won our undivided attention, and it's not long before she is extolling the virtues of what the Ritz Carlton can offer its guests.

"The classic Egyptian tour with the pyramids and Nile cruises is all fine, but you need to come here the week after to

recover," she explains. "Do some diving, laze on the beach, play some golf and just chill out. It's all here."

She is beginning to sell it to me. This is a most relaxing place, especially if you are one of those people who find the lounge floor as comfortable as the lounge furniture. Like most of the hotels we visit in Egypt, the Ritz Carlton features crash-out corners with rich red rugs littered with ornate cushions and leather poufs. These areas are perfect for flopping down after golf in the midday sun – and though initially viewed with curiosity, eventually become social focal points for our group.

From a golfing viewpoint, though, Sharm El Sheikh is not really up to spec. Bill Clinton and other luminaries may have stayed at the golf hotel here, but the course itself is a weak resort layout and certainly not up to the heady standards of Gary Player's Cascades creation, which is in the front rank of Egypt's golfing offensive.

And, finally, will that offensive succeed? Golf tour operator Peter Walton thinks so – his company Longshot has launched a special package here.

"It meets the four key criteria – courses; climate; accessibility and value for money," he says. "I know of nowhere in the world where you can play a course of the quality of Cascades for as little as £32."

True enough, But more importantly for me perhaps, there is nowhere in the world where you can experience 4,000 years of history in a single riverboat ride.

Golf Escapes **Morocco**

The snow-capped peaks of the Atlas mountain range tower over golfers at the Marrakech Royal Golf Club.

GOLF IN MOROCCO?

It's not as Bazaar as it sounds

It's cheaper than Portugal, more exotic than Spain and hotter than Italy. In golfing terms Morocco is a star in the making.

Words: **Stuart hood**

L et's be honest. Prior to this month the only thing I knew about Morocco was that my friend had once won £7,000 playing Blackjack there. But now I have found out, and whisper it quietly because mass tourism has yet to explode here, that Morocco is one of the world's up and coming golf destinations. And in terms of the course variety, volume and location all roads lead to Marrakech.

The Marrakech Royal is the most famous of the city's courses. A personal favourite of the late King Hassan II, the par 72 course weaves intimately between the local cypress, eucalyptus, and fruit trees. The course's backdrop is the Atlas Mountains, a snow-capped range so mesmeric in their beauty that on occasion they take your mind off the golf. And should your brain start to wander, at least one hole has the ability to punish your temerity. The 15th challenges golfers to hit their approach shots between a number of angled palm trees while avoiding the cavernous bunker hiding in the middle of two grassy mounds.

Undulating fairways and large greens provide the trademarks for the city's newest and most demanding course, The Amelkis. In prime condition throughout the year the course features a number of water hazards ready to swallow any wayward shots. And water is also the main danger on Marrakech's third layout.

Designed by Robert Trent Jones, The Palmeraie Golf Course has seven lakes in addition to the numerous waste bunkers and palm trees dotted around the 6,653 yard layout. The real star of the course, however, is the magnificently designed Moorish-style clubhouse, which forms the centrepiece of the whole resort.

Like most cosmopolitan cities, Marrakech possesses a centre, a heart if you will, where the city's diverse cultures come alive. London has Leicester Square, New York has Times Square, Paris has the Champs Elysses and Marrakech has the Djemaa-El-Fna.

By day the bustling local market tempts customers with its seemingly endless array of spices, cosmetics, carpets and silks. By night this huge square beats with

Brightly clothed drummers add to the unique atmosphere in the capital Marrakech's main square.

the hubbub and hullabaloo of open-air food stalls; non-stop acrobats; fire-eaters; snake-charmers; magicians; and native storytellers. And if the big city gets too much for you, Marrakech is nicknamed 'the gateway to the desert', so the peace, quiet and spectacular scenery exclusive to the Sahara is only a short journey away. Accommodation is the usual mixed bag with the city's Amelkis and Palmeraie courses integrated within luxury complexes. These resorts are seen as central to the Moroccan government's ambitious plans to increase the number of tourists visiting the country from three million to 10 million by 2010. The drive is focussing on the diversity of Morocco's tourism products and the country's appeal as a year round holiday destination.

"Morocco is about more than just Marrakech," says the Moroccan National Tourist Organisation's UK & Ireland director Ali El Kasmi. "We want tourists to become more familiar with Morocco's other cities and also the wide range of activities we cater for, including golf."

Six more purpose built resorts are planned for the next decade with golf likely to form an integral part of the infrastructure at each site. The first of these is already under construction just north of Agadir. The Taghazout resort will include 23,000 tourist beds and offer guests the chance to lose themselves in the local lifestyle at a purpose built fishing village and medina.

As managing director of specialist tour operator, Action Travel, Mohammed Fakir explains this all forms part of catering for the needs of golfers and non-golfers alike. "A lot of golfers like to travel with their spouses or family but want to be assured that others in the group will not find themselves short of things to do." he says.

Finding activities out with golf has never been a problem in Agadir. Morocco's most popular beach resort enjoys an average of 300 days sunshine a year. And, unless you are unlucky enough to pick one of the nine weeks the clouds come out, a feast of watersports, sunbathing and deep-sea fishing awaits. On the golfing front two sites featuring four nine-hole courses are already in position with a third venue set to open some time next year.

Three of the current courses exist within the Dunes Club. These layouts are graded on a difficulty scale so you can enjoy the game, whatever your level. The blue course is ideal for beginners, with the uphill 8th providing the most fearsome test. A steep climb ends at a hilltop green where suddenly the past few minutes of physical exertion seem worth it when you are greeted with a beautifully unblemished view of Agadir's Inezgane suburb. Yellow is aimed at testing mid-handicappers and the red course offers the sternest golfing examination, with the narrow uphill par-five 9th providing a sting in the tail.

Marrakech and Agadir make nice starters but Morocco's golfing main course comes in the governmental capital of Rabat. Home to a European Challenge Tour event and the prestigious King Hassan II trophy the Red Course at Dar Es Salam course is, plainly speaking, a wee bit special. It's one of these places that provoke endless arguments about what makes it so spectacular. Is it the true golfing test set by the course? Is it the seemingly infinite array of trees and flowers? Or is it the pink flamingos that hover majestically in the sky above? It's up to you to decide your personal favourite but each has its own special hook.

In terms of the course, accurate driving is essential and water an almost constant menace. The par three ninth is especially fraught with danger. At just under 190 yards it may look fairly innocuous on paper, but in reality a nerve-racking carry over water needs to be negotiated before sanctuary can be found on the green. The overall difficulty of the layout should not be underestimated and only the competent golfer should book a tee time. Last year's Challenge Tour event saw only five professionals finish under par, so those, like myself, can only dream of having their game described as competent need not apply. We should probably settle for the equally well conditioned, but less strenuous, blue and green courses, the latter comprising a mere nine holes.

When night falls a dazzling mixture of

Rabat's Islamic and European influences light up the walled city, making it a pleasant place to find a cosy bar, sip the local brew and watch the world go by. Rabat also has the advantage of being close to a couple of other tourist hotspots. The old imperial city of Fez, home of the traditional hat, is a couple of hours away and if the you fancy dusting down your Humphrey Bogart impression, Casablanca and a certain gin joint are a mere 90 minutes drive.

Still cynical about a golfing holiday to Morocco? Well consider these indisputable facts. Morocco has an average of 300 days sunshine a year. Over 20 top quality courses now exist across the length and breadth of the country. Regular services are available from London with a flying time of less than three hours. So it's cheap, easily accessible, varied and family friendly. In other words: perfect.

Carpets galore in a traditional Moroccan market.

THE MAIN COURSES

Royal Dar Es Salam Red Course, Rabat
Tel: 00 212 37 75 58 64
Par: 73 (7,307 yards)
Designer: Robert Trent Jones
What to expect: A complete golfing experience. An extremely challenging course set in the midst of stunning natural beauty.

Marrakech Royal Golf Club
Tel: 00 212 44 40 47 05
Par: 72
Designer: the pasha of Marrakech
What to expect: A short, intimate course weaving between a variety of cork and eucalyptus trees.

Palmeraie Golf Club, Marrakech
Tel: 00 212 44 30 10 10
Par: 72 (6,653 yards)
Designer: Robert Trent Jones
What to expect: Lots of water hazards, lots of bunkers and one hell of a clubhouse,

Amelkis Golf Club, Marrakech
Tel: 00 212 44 40 44 14
Par: 72 (7,128 yards)
Designer: Cabell B. Robinson
What to expect: Well-conditioned resort course with large greens and undulating fairways.

Dunes Golf Club Red Course, Agadir
Tel: 00 212 48 83 46 90
Par: 36 (3,335 yards)
Designer: Cabell B. Robinson
What to expect: An eclectic nine holes played in the shadow of a eucalyptus forest.

Turkish delight

The Turkish winter is mild and offers a pleasant climate for a golf break.

You'll find a high standard of golf course in Turkey.

Turkey may be the next major destination for British golfers searching for outstanding courses and fine hotels at reasonable costs. Thousands of UK players travel abroad every year, seeking new courses to conquer. Most will go to France, Spain, Portugal and the USA, but now there is a new European destination attracting their attention. It is Turkey, which is just under four hours flying distance away.

Turkey is new to golf but the game is not a totally new concept to the Turks. In fact, golf has been played here for more than a century. The Istanbul Golf Club, Turkey's first, opened in 1894. The course is still there but you will struggle to get a game as play is limited to members and their guests.

Instead of waiting for their invites, since 1994 visiting golfers have been able to bypass the ancient capital altogether and head for the Mediterranean. That was the year Belek's National Golf Club opened its gates. It has since established itself as Turkey's finest course.

Thankfully, for holidaying golfers, more courses quickly sprang up in its wake. Now the country boasts eight courses – five excellent ones in Belek plus another one which opened in September 2003, and there are more on the cards.

The key to Belek's success – apart from the sun and sea – is the quality of its hotels. They claim to offer some of the

From stunning swimming pools, fountains and water slides, as well as a busy street life, there's much to see and do for holidaymakers in Turkey.

most affordable five-star quality you will find, which means you will not go short of things to do. Jacuzzis, spas, gyms, tennis courts, theatres and even cinemas are common, while many boast their own Turkish baths (a must while you're there), and all seem to have tried to out-do their neighbours in creating the ultimate swimming pool.

Belek is a small place and the population is greatly swelled by the influx of tourists. Most of the central streets have been taken over by shops selling cheap 'designer' clothes. It's a long way from the electric atmosphere of an Istanbul bazaar, but there's still some fun to be had from the requisite bartering.

There are some excellent five star hotels situated along the sea-front offering magnificent facilities. Gloria Golf Resort, Sirene Golf Hotel Palace and Village and Nobilis have their own fine golf courses attached. When you meet up in the bar in the evening, stick around, instead of heading by taxi for town, stay and be entertained, wined and dined at the excellent hotels.

Getting back to the golf, the peak season in Turkey runs from the middle of September to the beginning of June. It's when the temperatures are lower and the prices higher. Remember to take a current handicap certificate and put soft spikes on your golf shoes.

Millenium Driving Range and Golf School has just recently opened in Antalya town, which is within a few minutes distance from the Dedeman and Talya Hotels, boasting excellent practice facilities to business-men visiting Antalya and also offering group or individual teaching facilities.

"The peak season for golf in Turkey runs from the middle of September to the beginning of June. This is when the temperatures are lower"

Check out the courses in Belek

Gloria Golf Club

Living up to its name, Gloria is a lush, glorious course. There is a little more room off the tee than at the National GC, but the fairways are lined with pine trees, so accuracy is still important. Four lakes come into play with the largest encroaching play on the 4th, 13th and 14th holes. You can really make a mess of a good round on the par three 13th where there is water right up to the putting surface. Survive this and you have to tackle the 14th where the wet stuff threatens both your tee shot and approach. Take plenty of balls. Open for just a year, the nine-hole Verde course has given Gloria a much needed boost in the fact of mounting demand for tee times. Designed along similar lines to the original 18 holes, Gloria Verde can provide a perfectly respectable 18-hole challenge of its own – each hole has two sets of tees – or combine effectively with either of the older nines. The fairways are carved through the pines and there is one substantial water hazard which comes into play most prominently on the par four third where the approach shot needs a 100-yard carry.

National Golf Club

Along the lines of a South Carolina layout, this is generally regarded as Turkey's finest course. It hosted the Turkish Seniors Open in 1996 and 1997 and is a difficult but fair test. The holes wind through pine and eucalyptus trees and are tight in places. Water is a feature, particularly on the par three 2nd, the tricky par five 4th and the 18th where a large lake threatens a hook off the tee before curving in front of the green to capture a weak approach. The National was ranked 16th best golf course in the world by an American golf publication.

Nobilis Golf Club

Nobilis is built on the site of a Roman settlement and is probably the most resort-like of Belek's courses. None of the original ruins remain, although there are some fake crumblings and a clubhouse full of every Roman flourish imaginable. The course is fairly flat with fewer trees than its neighbour, Gloria, but there is plenty to interest golfers of all standards. The 11th hole is a tricky par five with room to open the shoulders off the tee

and set up the opportunity to fire one over the water that cuts in from the right about 100 yards from the green. You can expect a course in superb condition.

Tat Golf International GC

There is nothing tatty about these 27 holes. Tatbeach differs in style to Belek's other courses. The land here is more hilly and the layout more varied. Several holes are near the sea and these have something of a links feel with their undulating fairways. The holes that play directly towards the Mediterranean are a difficult test, particularly if the wind blows. If you like your holiday golf to have an edge you won't be disappointed here.

Antalya Golf Club

The most ambitious golf facility in Belek, Antalya Golf Club has already made a considerable impact on the region's visitors. It consists of two 18-hole courses – the Pasha, which opened in November 2002, and Sultan, which opened in September 2003. Both have been constructed by European Golf Design, a subsidiary of the PGA European Tour, under the personal supervision of Northern Irish professional David Jones. One of the triumphs of the Pasha is how the designers have eked out a worthy 18-hole challenge, complete with four par-five holes, from what appears to be a little more than half the land which has been devoted to the Sultan.

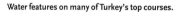

Water features on many of Turkey's top courses.

FULL CIRCLE
The World Golf Village is built around
a lake. This is the view from the
'Tower Shrine', the lofty peak that
forms its centrepiece.

The world capital of
golf

The World Golf Village is the kind of place where golf's biggest names drop in for a clinic – or even a few holes. So what's the big attraction? And what kind of base does it make for a golf holiday? Duncan Lennard reports from Florida.

Photography: **Angus Murray**

BIG NAMES, BIG TEST
Arnold Palmer and Jack Nicklaus joined forces to design the King & the Bear. Prepare for a test worthy of two multi-major winners.

W hen I arrive, Jack Nicklaus and Arnold Palmer are opening their new golf course. Sam Snead is about to give a clinic. Juli Inkster and Roberto de Vicenzo are busy winning a Seniors & Ladies tournament. And eight golfing heroes are preparing to be inducted into the game's official Hall of Fame. Whichever way I turn, there seems to be a legend of golf.

But this is just an ordinary week at the World Golf Village in Jacksonville, Florida. Okay, perhaps the fame quota is a little higher than average just now – but this is a place where the big names seem to drop in for laughs.

Unable to split myself into four parts, I plump for Snead's clinic. A crowd of 200 or so locals has gathered to watch the 88-year-old seven-time major winner. He's been here only five minutes, but already they are in stitches.

"I've played with four presidents," warbles the great man. "First time I played with President Eisenhower he was standing up too straight as he swung. I said to him: 'Mr President, you gotta stick your ass out.' Two men ran up and yelled 'Jeez, don't you realise that's the President you're talking to?' I said: 'He's still got an ass hasn't he?'"

Snead's clinic involves the swatting of half a dozen balls with his still-rhythmic swing, plus a rich crop of anecdotes from his life in golf.

"I had no money when I started," he says. "I had to stay in some pretty cheap hotels. You know you're in a cheap hotel when you ring down to reception and say: 'I've got a leak in the sink,' and they reply: 'Go on then, if you must.'"

Snead's presence confirms the World Golf Village as a mecca for star-spotters, and it makes a superb centrepiece for a golf holiday in north east Florida. The village sits right next to the mighty I-95 interstate, a north-south dual carriageway that should really be rechristened the Golf Highway. The road is bordered by trees, through which you can see a never-ending series of green-gold fairways and twinkling lakes.

This corner of Florida, encompassing the towns of Jacksonville and St Augustine, finds space for a remarkable

WHERE TO PLAY

The Courses
Plenty more to choose from, but these should be top of your playlist.

3: THE KING & THE BEAR

At the World Golf Village, Jacksonville
7,279 yards, par 72
Designers Jack Nicklaus and Arnold Palmer.
Character There is scarcely a divot in this new course, sculpted by Arnie and Jack themselves. Fairways slope and shelve around lakes galore, and rocks on the borders add to the attractive look. Not for beginners, though five tee settings allow most to enjoy a challenging layout.
Signature hole Any on the front nine, which features gently rolling fairways and attempts a Scottish-style feel. It doesn't succeed, but this is still a great front nine.
Call 001 904 940 6200.

2: THE SLAMMER & THE SQUIRE

At the World Golf Village, Jacksonville
6,940 yards, par 72
Designers Bobby Weed, with Gene Sarazen and Sam Snead.
Character The home of the Legends of Golf event on the US Seniors Tour, this course has two distinct nines. The front nine is in the trees, while the back looks like the set of *Waterworld*. Not too penal off the tee, but green contouring makes scoring tough.
Signature hole The 4th, a par-5 which curves gently to the right before ducking back sharply left. The green is set back against the water.
Call 001 904 940 6100.

1: GOLF CLUB OF JACKSONVILLE

6,620 yards, par 71
Designers Bobby Weed and Mark McCumber.
Character A good value course with more character than many Florida layouts. Untouched marshland borders the holes, giving the place a more natural feel than some. More room off the tee than other courses, but generous dollops of pine and water keep the quality of test pretty high.
Signature hole The 6th, a par-5 dogleg right with water hazards right and left. A good drive tempts you to have a crack in two. The green is well protected by mounds and sand.
Call 001 904 779 0800.

4: TOURNAMENT PLAYERS CLUB

Sawgrass
Stadium Course 6,954 yards, par 72
Valley Course 6,838 yards, par 71
Designer Pete Dye.
Character 36 holes to convince you that all golfers are masochists. Both courses are extremely cruel, but give a lot of pleasure too. The island green 17th on the Stadium epitomises the design – spectacular, artificial and frightening. You've two ways of playing here – by staying at the Marriott Hotel (call 001 904 285 7777) to become an associate member.
Signature hole It can only be the 17th – 132 yards to an island green. Pros like Nick Price say it's the reason the Players Championship will never be a major; but no hole has more impact.
Call 001 904 273 3233.

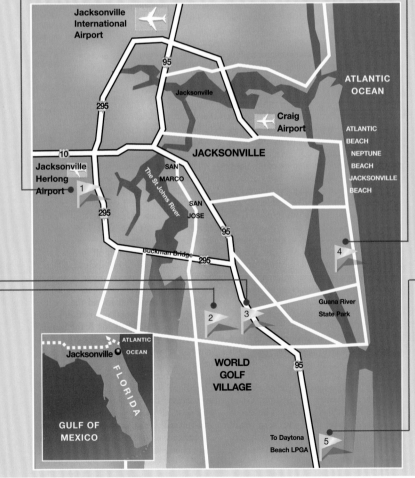

Jacksonville
International
Airport

95

295

Jacksonville

Craig
Airport

ATLANTIC
OCEAN

10

JACKSONVILLE

ATLANTIC
BEACH

NEPTUNE
BEACH

JACKSONVILLE
BEACH

Jacksonville
Herlong
Airport

1

SAN
MARCO

The St. Johns River

SAN
JOSE

295

95

Buckman Bridge 295

4

2   3

Guana River
State Park

Jacksonville

ATLANTIC
OCEAN

F L O R I D A

WORLD
GOLF
VILLAGE

95

GULF OF
MEXICO

To Daytona
Beach LPGA

5

5: LPGA INTERNATIONAL

Daytona Beach
Champions Course 7,088 yards, par 72
Legends Course 6,984 yards, par 72
Designers Rees Jones and Arthur Hills.
Character The LPGA headquarters features two perfectly conditioned 18-hole courses and superb practice facilities. Don't expect them to look natural – almost all the mounding is artificial – but do expect spectacular shotmaking opportunities and very fast greens.
Signature hole On the Champions Course the 5th, a mid-length par-5 with water threatening down the right from tee to green. On the Legends Course, the 11th is a challenging 400-yarder with water and well-placed traps.
Call 001 904 274 6200.

53 courses, including the famed Tournament Players Club at Sawgrass, home of the Players Championship. What's more, both the USPGA and LPGA Tours have decided to base their headquarters in the area. Mix in the Golf Village itself, and you have a part of the globe that has willingly surrendered to the world's greatest sport.

The World Golf Village is five years old, and designed in a circle, around a lake. Out in the water is a replica green of the 17th at Sawgrass, and for a couple of bucks you can take on the shot from a teeing ground on the edge. Elsewhere there is an enormous PGA Tour retail outlet, a host of other shops, a bar owned by Caddyshack star Bill Murray, another owned by Mr Snead, the plush Renaissance Hotel, and a putting course. The path round the lake is grandly titled the 'Walk of Champions' – its paving stones inscribed, Hollywood-style, with the biggest signatures in golf.

But the Village's chief attraction is the Hall of Fame. This actually comprises four halls on two levels. In the first, a giant TV screen dominates. A film about the glories of golf entitled 'Passion to Play' runs continuously. Lining the walls are huge pictures of famous golfers, accompanied by quotes from Hall-of-Famers like Bobby Jones.

"Golf is usually played with the outward appearance of great dignity," Jones apparently said. "It is nevertheless a game of considerable passion, either the explosive type or that which burns inwardly and sears the soul."

The room tries to capture the essence of golf – perhaps an unwise thing to do with a game whose mystery is its chief attraction.

Further in, I find the first exhibit. It is the 6-iron used by Alan Shepard for his famous moon shot in 1971. "Did you know a 250-yard drive on earth would go 1,500 yards on the moon?" Shepard's recorded voice asks. Well no Alan, now you mention it, I didn't. Shepard goes on to admit that his first effort on the moon resulted in a shank. A TV screen replays his lunar lunging, and it is compulsive viewing.

I climb the stairs to be greeted by a guy who hands me a walkie-talkie. "Take this," he says, "It's an Acoustiguide." God bless America.

The Acoustiguide guides me acoustically round the first of the upstairs halls, dedicated to the history of the game. Scottish bagpipes wheeze merrily but naffly as I walk across a life-size replica of the Swilcan Bridge.

A large green dominates the room, rough underfoot to simulate Scottish greens of yore. I am encouraged to jump on and have a putt, using a replica 19th century putter and balls. Also in the room is an impressive collection of old clubs, including a huge shovel of a wedge called the Hendry & Bishop Giant Cardinal Niblick, circa 1910. The face is round and about the size of a small dinner plate. Clearly oversize clubs are nothing new. Despite the bagpipes, there's a lot to see here.

The next room is the Hall of Fame itself. It is big, bright and minimalist. The Hall contains nothing but an arcing series of plinths, each one dedicated to an inductee. But behind these is perhaps the building's most interesting exhibit. Inductees have donated possessions to the Hall of Fame, and they have been collated behind thick, thick glass in a wall display. Remember Seve's great chip to the holeside at the last at Lytham in '88? The sand-wedge he used is here. So is the glove Arnie used in winning the '62 US Open – and it is huge. Augusta founder Clifford Roberts' Green Jacket hangs next to it. But perhaps best of all is Sam Snead's childhood lunchbox, which he took to school every day. His inscribed name is still visible on the edge.

The final hall is dedicated to the modern game. Another green sprawls across the floor, this one faster. An invisible crowd roars every time you knock in a putt. Shrines to the PGA and LPGA come next, and last of all is a golf simulator which compares your swing with the greats. Apparently mine is like Gary Player's. I'm sure he'll be delighted. Closer examination reveals the comparison is based on speed of swing rather than clubface position at impact.

The Village has two 18-hole courses. The Slammer & the Squire was, as its name suggests, designed by Snead and Gene Sarazen. See if you can guess who created the new The King & the Bear Course (clue in the first line of this article).

Angie Rodriguez is golf pro at the Village. She says: "The Slammer & the Squire is a good resort course, designed for the resort player. From tee to green it's not very hard, but round the greens you need to know what you're doing. It's fun and playable. The King & the Bear is longer and a little tougher on the long game. The two courses complement each other."

While that's true, both are typically Floridian – artificial, water-ridden, immaculate and full of exciting target golf shots to receptive greens. A bump-and-run will be as much use to you as a chocolate golf ball. And unless you're a club champion, bring a lofted fairway wood – you'll need it for the inevitable series of long approach shots into well-protected putting surfaces.

It's time to leave the confines of the Golf Village and explore the wider world beyond. What strikes me is that the Jacksonville region as a whole is also archetypal Florida. Flat as the green of your dreams, it consists of swamps, lagoons and pine forests. It is also as commercial as the rest of this nation. The never-ending sequence of billboards along the I-95 (many advertising golf courses) tells you all about that.

The World Golf Village is almost equidistant from the LPGA headquarters, to the south at Daytona Beach, and the USPGA Tour's base at Sawgrass. Both have 36 holes surrounding them, and both are worth a look for the holidaying golfer. Getting a game on the famous Stadium Course at Sawgrass, however, can set you ' back $610 (£422). That's because the only way you can play there is by staying at the local Marriott Hotel, where rooms cost up to $300. The green fee alone reaches $310 in peak season. On the other hand, go at the right time and you can get hotel and golf for $254 (£175).

The strange thing is, even at that price the course is just about worth it. I'm not normally a fan of artificial layouts, especially ones that cost nearly 200 quid, but this is a course that arrogantly states "man can do a better job than nature," and pretty much carries it off.

Fans of the Players Championship will know the colour scheme – ivory bunkers, jade fairways and sapphire ponds. The condition looks like Augusta on a good day. Perched fairways slope crazily down to alligator-infested water. Bunkers stretch from tee to green. Pins stand defiantly on tiny green plateaux. Holes are dwarfed by unapologetic mounding. It is a 21st century golf course and requires a space-age game.

The two courses at the LPGA base come at a friendlier price. Although they lack the drama of Sawgrass, they offer great tests, plus greens where a 15-footer hit on-line will stay on-line.

Away from these locations, there are another 50 courses within an hour's drive to choose from. Nowhere in the world offers you more opportunities, as the late great Bobby Jones put it, to explode or to sear inwardly.

THE ULTIMATE GOLF SHOP
The PGA Tour Shop is a massive 30,000 square feet, each one crammed with golf's newest equipment.

Planning your trip

When to go
■ The climate is good all year round. Consider travelling either during Players Championship week (March); during the Seniors Tour Legends tournament (end of March), or in Hall of Fame induction week (November). Chances are you'll bump into some big names.

Golf packages
■ The American Golf Holiday will tailor a package to suit you; call 02380 465885.

PITCHERS AT AN EXHIBITION
Ancient wedges feature in a display in the Golf Hall of Fame. The Hall is split into four rooms and 18 separate exhibits.

Golf hints
■ Rubber cleats are *de rigeur*. Booking your round in good time means you can pick your time and avoid the heat of the day. When you book, check what is included. Most prices include buggies and some include range balls. Mozzies can be a bother, so invest in some repellent. Consider packing a lob wedge for thick greenside rough shots onto fast putting surfaces.

Away from the course
■ 12 miles to the east of Jacksonville are white sand beaches. At Jacksonville Beach is Adventure Landing, which features two 18-hole miniature golf courses, batting cages, a go-cart track, 100 arcade games, Shipwreck Island water park and the Rage, Florida's only uphill water coaster. Jacksonville itself has museums, theatres, parks and waterfront shopping arcades.

St Augustine, down the coast, is supposedly where Florida was named and claimed for Spain by Ponce de Leon. The Spaniard also believed he had discovered the Fountain of Youth here, and you can still guzzle from it today. Don't expect the gift of eternal life, though – shortly afterwards Ponce died from a poison arrow in the stomach.

The Mild Wild West

With $10 million courses and luxurious clubhouses, the West isn't as wild as it used to be. But those looking for a unique and rigorous challenge will still find what they're looking for in the desert. Golf World sent its own scout Tony Dear to Arizona to investigate.

Roadrunners don't really say 'beep, beep'. Nor do they frustrate dumb coyotes planning to blow them up. In fact, they're not nearly as composed and smart as the Warner Bros would have us believe. The spread of golf in the USA's south-western deserts, and Southern Arizona's Sonoran Desert in particular, has left Geococyxx Califorianus anxiously looking over his shoulder for silver haired retirees from Michigan bombing about the place on battery driven golf carts.

Twenty-five years ago it was a very different story. With most of the Grand Canyon State's 125 courses confined to urban areas the roadrunner had the area surrounding Phoenix and Tucson virtually to himself. The desert was a harsh place covered in nothing but sand, cacti and rocks.

Much of it still is, of course, but the land is slowly changing colour. Some of what was once a dirty yellow has now become a rich and vibrant green. And where lonesome cowboys once rode off into the sunset on horseback, greenkeepers now scurry about at sunrise on the back of lawnmowers.

There are now well over 300 courses in Arizona. Scottsdale, Phoenix's most affluent suburb, has been the focus for much of the construction and it was here that the first genuine desert golf course, Desert Highlands, was built. Funded by mega bucks property developer Lyle Anderson and designed in 1980 by Jack Nicklaus and Bob Cupp, it introduced target golf to the world and was the first course where natural desert terrain between the holes was kept intact. Not only did it look good, it preserved much of the natural ecosystem and saved a lot of water too. So even the hippies and

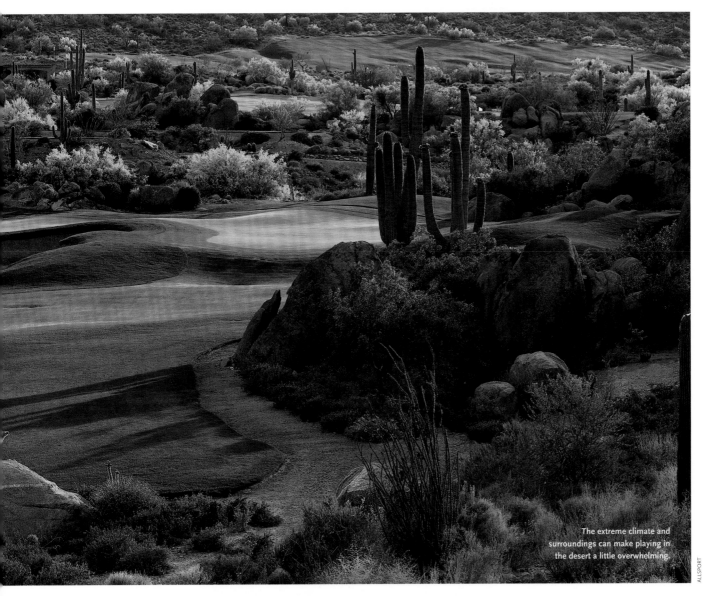

The extreme climate and surroundings can make playing in the desert a little overwhelming.

ALLSPORT

" Desert Highlands in Scottsdale introduced target golf to the world, and was the first course where natural desert terrain between the holes was kept in tact "

conservationists were happy.

The few that weren't so keen criticised the one dimensional design of the course, saying it forced you to play a hole a certain way. They had a point but even they couldn't deny desert golf was a worthy addition to the game's diverse mix of challenges. The Bear was rightly proud of the result and maintains it is some of his best ever work. As for Cupp,

he hit the nail on the head when he described it as "the course that changed Arizona golf".

It wasn't long before Scottsdale was established as the place to come for golfers wanting that authentic desert experience. Two decades on, nothing has changed. Southern California, the area around Las Vegas and parts of New Mexico, have desert layouts of their own

but none of them can boast the profusion of cacti and wildlife you get at courses in and around Scottsdale. Desert golf here is the real deal.

Thirteen million people now come every year to plot a route between the Saguaros. They may not get the chance to tee it up at Desert Highlands (playing rights come with the purchase of a house on the property – the cheapest is $600,000) but they can play a number of other great desert courses that are ranked in America's top 100. Sunridge Canyon, Troon North, Grayhawk, the TPC of Scottsdale and Talking Stick are fabulous

Grayhawk, one of Scottsdale's premier courses, can prove to be very challenging.

❝ Desert golf courses look inviting in the pictures but easy and prone to low scoring they are not. You have to strike your approach shots high and with great precision ❞

tracks all of which offer the public that trip into the unknown.

With developers restricted to turfing just 90 acres of land, houses, villas and condos bordering some of the fairways can dilute the experience and give holes a contrived feel. But most of the time the golfer will be out in the open with just his partners, the cacti and the often brutally hot sun for company.

For the first-timer the alien combination of extreme climate and surroundings can make playing in the desert a bit overwhelming. The greens are invariably rock hard and to hold them you have to strike your approach shot high and with great precision. That means you must find the fairway off the tee. But this is target golf at its purest, where a sort of golfing hopscotch is played and the penalty for missing a number can be severe. Should you carve your ball out into the scrub one of two things will happen to it. It will either avoid the sparse undergrowth altogether and trickle out into a bare, sandy lie from where you might be able to poke a short iron back on to the fairway. Or it will get lodged in something thick, wild and ugly

from where there is no hope of escape. Either way, you probably ain't gonna make a par. Yes, desert golf courses look inviting in pictures but easy and prone to low scoring they are not. The Pinnacle Course at Troon North, for instance, is so tough it has been called a 'right Sonora bitch'.

The best time to see how low you can go is in winter when the mercury hovers around the 70-degree mark. By May the temperature is well into the 90s and in July, when it can get as high as 120, only the truly committed, or rather those who should be committed, are to be found swinging a golf club. Some courses even have buggies with drizzle pipes that emit a fine spray of water and there's always the drinks cart. But no matter how many iced beverages you consume or how damp you make yourself with the drizzle pipe, you'll never escape the feeling you are playing golf in an oven.

Visiting at this time of year does have its compensations though. Because tour parties are thin on the ground and even the locals are holed up inside with the air conditioning set to high, green fees come tumbling down. Range balls, a buggy, a

pitch-mark repairer, a yardage book and a bag tag are included in the green fee, but it's still a lot of green for not many greens, so to speak. In summer you get all the above for alot less, a steal considering the quality of the course. Similarly at Sunridge Canyon, the winter green fee is cut by more than half on June 3rd.

If you can survive the mid-summer heat, you'll usually find a course in every bit as good condition as it was back in January. Most of the upscale courses in Scottsdale feature PenCross greens. This Bent grass produces quick and beautifully smooth putting surfaces and, although more suited to a cooler climate, it can survive the Arizona summer with intensive greenkeeping and reduced traffic. Jay Haffner, director of golf at Sunridge Canyon, explains: "We get 36,000 rounds a year but two thirds of them are in winter. The greens are at their best then but they are still as good as most in the country in the summer. The grass can become a bit thin and weak in July and August but with relatively few golfers out there it stays alive." Twenty-eight greenstaff and an

Most of the time you will be out in the open with just your partners and the cacti for company.

Strange but true. Water features on many of the desert courses.

" If you can survive the mid-summer heat, you'll usually find a course in great condition. And there'll be fewer people out on the course at that time of year "

annual maintenance budget of $1.2 million helps as well, of course, as does two million gallons of water a day. They may require less water than nearby parkland courses of a similar acreage but that's not to say desert courses don't like a drink. "We've been open for seven years and have just used our one billionth gallon of water," says Haffner. "It's reclaimed and piped from the water treatment plant in nearby Fountain Hills. We pay $250,000 a year for it."

At the TPC of Scottsdale, head superintendent Chuck Green says his greens are just as good in summer as they are in winter when they come under the spotlight during the Phoenix Open. "Unlike some of the other courses around here we have Tifdwarf Bermuda greens. It's perfectly adapted for use in the South. Bermuda grass loves the heat so it flourishes during July and August. In October, when it starts going dormant, we overseed it with Poa-Trivialis to maintain the green colour." Chuck has 50

Troon North has several immoveable objects.

staff at his disposal (there are two courses) and just over $2.5 million to spend, "of which $400,000 goes on water," he says.

Even the local munis remain green and attractive all year round. Papago, surely one of the world's best publicly owned courses, benefits from a maintenance budget of roughly $1 million year. Dobson Ranch in nearby Mesa spends an additional $500,000 to keep its 18 holes looking good. How many munis in

Expect to see

Most desert creatures are nocturnal but if you have an early tee time you may still spot some.

ROADRUNNER

Famous for foiling coyote attempts to catch them in cartoons, they're actually very nervous and scamper off as soon as your buggy comes into view. They often eat rattlesnakes and have a top speed of 17mph.

COYOTE

Actually it's the coyote with the brains. They're far more likely to catch a roadrunner than have a 1000lb anvil dropped on their head by one. Very shy, coyotes are rarely seen on golf courses during the hours of daylight.

RATTLESNAKE

Likely to slink away at the first sign of trouble. If you see one that's coiled up and rattling, our advice is to run away very fast. If you hit your ball into the desert in summer it might be a good idea to leave it out there.

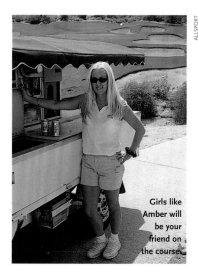

ALLSPORT

Girls like Amber will be your friend on the course.

There are over 125 courses in the Grand Canyon State.

Britain have resources anything like as generous?

Perfect playing conditions and 320 days of sunshine are a pretty attractive combination for the desert golfer. But the good stuff doesn't end there. This is the USA where bag drop boys take your clubs to your buggy and clean them when you're done. This is where a bucket of range balls is included in the green fee and the grass you hit off on the range is in better condition than the grass on the fairways at your home club. This is the country where a GPS guidance system in every buggy is fast becoming the norm, at expensive courses at least. And this is where the golfer needn't go hungry or

> ❝ Looking good (tall, blond and tanned) and acting professionally can earn a cart girl over $1,000 a weekend, about 30% of which is made up of tips ❞

thirsty for long because the drinks cart, laden with bottled water, beers, soft drinks, chocolate bars, sandwiches and thick Cuban cigars, is never more than a hole or two away.

Operating the drinks cart at a high-end golf club in America is a position of some responsibility. "The cart girl is a valued member of staff. She deals with the paying public as much as, if not more than, the guys in the pro shop or restaurant. So she has to look good and act professionally," says Haffner.

Looking good (tall, blond, tanned) and acting professionally can earn the cart girl over $1,000 a weekend, about

30% of which is made up of tips, although one 'cart tart' who worked at a well-known club in Scottsdale did once bank $120,000 in a single year. Apparently, besides the more usual cold beer and crisps, her menu included certain 'extras'. Eventually, the members' wives got wind and the girl was dismissed on the spot.

The West isn't as wild as it once was but playing golf in the desert is still a tough proposition. You won't be fired at by Red Indians but you may find yourself coming off what looked like a pretty straightforward course with a 97 and asking yourself 'HOW?'

Top 10 desert courses in Arizona you can play

2.	TPC of Scottsdale (Stadium), Scottsdale.
3.	Sunridge Canyon, Fountain Hills.
4.	Troon North (Pinnacle), Scottsdale.
5.	Gold Canyon (Dinosaur), Gold Canyon.
6.	Grayhawk (Talon), Scottsdale.
7.	Legend Trail, Scottsdale.
8.	Golf Club at Vistoso, Tucson.
9.	Ventana Canyon, Tucson.
10.	Talking Stick (North).

Myrtle Beach magic

Words: **Ann Harper** Photography: **Bob Atkins**

It's widely regarded as the golfing capital of America. And when you consider there are over 100 courses to choose from, it's easy to see why Myrtle Beach is the best.

Words: **Anne Harper**
Photography: **Bob Atkins**

f you want too much of everything on a holiday…go to America. If you want too much of everything on a golf holiday…go to Myrtle Beach. This 100-square mile stretch of lush, wooded South Carolina lowland, with more than 120 golf courses, has it all.

All this golfing fervour runs along a spectacular 60-mile stretch of golden crescent shaped beach, known as The Grand Strand. It stretches from the little creeks and fishing villages, which hug the North Carolina state line, to the gracious old pink-washed Georgetown down in the south.

Official figures support the claim of 120 golf courses, along with hundreds of hotels and in excess of 2,000 restaurants. As they keep building and adding to this list almost by the day, those figures are probably way out of date even before you read this feature.

Myrtle Beach has been a favourite destination for generations of Americans and at its heart still lies its Blackpoolesque seaside town of white knuckle rides, tattoo parlours, and candy floss. But if it's golf you want…look no further.

The Grand Strand offers the most fantastic array of golf courses on earth from testing links over scenic salt marshes, through to steady parkland golf and stunning layouts trailing across the old rice and indigo plantations of the Deep South. This rich heritage – for Myrtle Beach once produced enough rice to feed America – is reflected in the names of the clubs such as Indigo Creek, Pawley's Plantation, Indian Wells and Marsh Harbour.

Myrtle Beach can also boast some of the greatest names in golf behind their fantastic array of courses. The credits run like an Oscar winning movie with superstar architects such as Jack Nicklaus, Greg Norman, Robert Trent Jones, Tom Fazio, Gary Player, Arnold Palmer, Sam Snead…the list rolls on endlessly.

For those wanting to sharpen up their golfing skills there are numerous golf schools and academies with top teaching professionals. And everywhere you are greeted with that matchless US standard of service, starting with the bag drop and ending with your last Tequila Sunrise in the bar. You don't even need to take clubs with you as you can hire top brands for the duration of your stay. When it comes to putting the customer first, no-one, just no-one, does it like the Americans.

It doesn't matter if you're a weekend hacker or the club champion, Myrtle Beach has a golf course that appeals to all types of golfer. But you do need to decide where you want to base yourself as this is golf with burgers and rock 'n roll to go.

So if you're looking for a little Southern style gracious living with bluebirds on your porch and mint juleps in the rocking chair then it's best to base yourself on the south side of the resort where there's a quieter and more refined atmosphere. However, if you want excitement, then Myrtle Beach can party like there's no tomorrow, with clubs, bars, restaurants, theatres, live music venues and cafes galore.

Then there are its great shopping malls stacked to the rafters with the very best consumer goods. While if it's just good old fashioned family fun you're looking for, it's all on your doorstep with great attractions, including themed pitch and putt courses and adventure parks.

Last word has to go to Myrtle Beach Golf Holiday, which represents over 90 of the clubs with its stirring legend: "Only one game can create such insanity…and only one place can cater for it." It's Myrtle Beach – you got it!

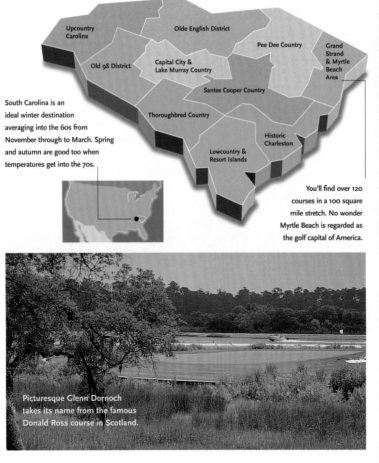

South Carolina is an ideal winter destination averaging into the 60s from November through to March. Spring and autumn are good too when temperatures get into the 70s.

Upcountry Carolina

Olde English District

Pee Dee Country

Grand Strand & Myrtle Beach Area

Old 98 District

Capital City & Lake Murray Country

Santee Cooper Country

Thoroughbred Country

Historic Charleston

Lowcountry & Resort Islands

You'll find over 120 courses in a 100 square mile stretch. No wonder Myrtle Beach is regarded as the golf capital of America.

Picturesque Glenn Dornoch takes its name from the famous Donald Ross course in Scotland.

You'll find all types of golf course at Myrtle Beach, especially ones with plenty of water hazards.

HOLIDAY 1 If you want...

A golf holiday for the family

Can you recommend a good place to stay for a family group?
Fun is Myrtle Beach's watchword, so you really can't go wrong. The Grand Strand offers families (and everybody) a safe, welcoming and relaxed holiday atmosphere. With children you want to be close to the action. One option is either The Hampton Inn or Fairfield Suites at Broadway at the Beach – the hub of most of the action with restaurants, speciality shops, an IMAX Theatre and Celebrity Square nightclub complex. If you prefer action and beach life try Ocean Boulevard, lined with big hotels facing onto the beautiful beach. The hotels often offer efficiencies – which are hotel rooms with small kitchens – ideal with families.

You mentioned the beach at Myrtle Beach. What's it like?
The beach itself is one of Myrtle Beach's great assets. It's long with golden sand and is clean and well supervised by qualified lifeguards and there are plenty of little restaurants close by so you can break off and take a leisurely lunch. Needless to say all the golf courses and the town's innumerable array of leisure activities are also close at hand. So you won't have to travel far to find the many attractions.

A walk down a typical Gerogetown street can be an enjoyable experience.

We would like to brush up on our golf while on holiday. Where can we get some lessons for both the adults and children in our party?
We need to take a lesson out of the US books when it comes to youngsters and golf. The clubs are very welcoming to families and there are some superb teaching academies staffed by top teaching professionals. Possum Trot Golf Club has a very friendly teaching academy with a varied curriculum and some of America's top instructors. They offer one, two and three-day schools from 9am to 3pm daily. There is also a three-day mini school from 9-12 noon.

We don't intend being on the golf course all week. Can you give us some ideas of what else there is to do for the whole family?
Broadway at the Beach – a mix of entertainment, shopping and dining, the alligator farm at Barefoot Landing or any of the excellent mini golf courses with names such as Jungle Lagoon, Pirates Watch and Buccaneer Bay.

Can you give us some tips on holidaying in Myrtle Beach?
Pack plenty of insect repellent when playing at dusk. Avoid the high summer if you don't like humidity as it can get high at these times.Take traveller's cheques or dollars instead of sterling as their banks do not like to handle pounds.

Affectionately known as "The Grandaddy", Pine Lakes is the original Myrtle Beach course built in 1927.

HOLIDAY 2 If you want...

A great society break

More than 120 courses! This sounds like a triumph of quantity over quality. Surely there's some very poor ones?
Myrtle Beach prides itself on being America's golfing capital and there's no room for really poor courses. You will be simply amazed by the variety and the quality of the golf here. Green fees do vary and the only rule of thumb is that the cost probably reflects the quality and layout of the course and the levels of customer service. However, you can get a really great golf experience and still pay a modest green fee.

Too many courses, too little time. We're only there for ten days. We're a varied handicap group but do take the game seriously. Can you suggest a few clubs to us?
Perhaps it's easier to go on groupings. Start with the Links Group, which owns 10 courses, including Cypress Bay, Indian Wells, Indigo Creek, Sea Gull and the premium priced International.
Barefoot Resort Golf has some big names behind their course collection each named after the architect. So we have the Fazio Course, the Love Course...and no prizes for guessing who's behind the Norman Course.
Myrtle Beach National has some wonderful courses with the Arnold Palmer-designed Kings North being their key course. This group offers a variety of courses with green fees for all budgets and also includes Litchfield. Myrtle Beach National and Aberdeen.

Burroughs and Chapin are the oldest landowners in Myrtle Beach and they own and manage four of the Grand Strand's finest in Tidewater, the acclaimed Grande Dunes and two at Myrtlewood – the Palmetto and Pine Hills.

And what about the nightlife? After a good day's golf we look forward to some good food, a few beers and on to a club. Any suggestions?
Night life in Myrtle Beach can be as tasteful or as tacky as you like. Myrtle Beach has over 2,000 restaurants and most of them are to be found at Restaurant Row. Here you'll find Sam Snead's

Tavern – set up by the golfing legend himself. It's very popular with golfers as it offers a varied menu at reasonable prices and you are just surrounded by memorabilia of the great man. Restaurant Row is also where you'll find three nightclubs in one with the 2001 Club. Or there's the Hard Rock Café – great for rockers and golfers and Hooters – a very blokeish place – with pretty girls in tee-shirts, serving (and flirting) at the tables. After this you could take in the House of Blues which has great live music every night and attracts some of the big names in rock and blues to its stage. Celebrity Square at Broadway at the Beach boasts the best party in town and offers a fantastic atmosphere with dozens of small bars, clubs and restaurants playing a mix of disco and live music and the party just spills out into the square.

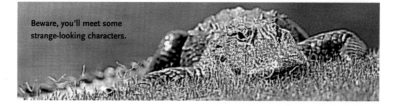

Beware, you'll meet some strange-looking characters.

Blackmoor Golf Club was Gary Player's first design in the Myrtle Beach area.

If you want...

A husband and wife trip

We do fancy Myrtle Beach as we've done Florida to death. But isn't it all a bit too much like Blackpool?
In central Myrtle Beach, yes, because it developed as a bright and breezy seaside town, but remember good old Blackpool has some

You must visit the Caledonia Golf Club...it's pure Gone With The Wind.

great golf close at hand too. If you head towards the North Carolina border or south of the town, you come across laid back fishing villages along salt creek inlets.

A curious thing about Myrtle Beach is that it doesn't have any five star hotels but if you're looking for somewhere with a touch of class and real South Carolina feel, try the Litchfield Resort on the south side. Guests have a choice of accommodation from hotel suites, ocean-front apartments and fairway cottages or villas.

Litchfield itself has three of the best courses along the Grand Strand. The Litchfield Country Club is a semi-private club created from an old rice plantation and with an old world feel. Its sister clubs are the Tom Jackson-designed River Club with its wide fairways, fast greens and stunning 18th hole and the Willbrook, created by Dan Maples from two old rice plantations and offers a lovely unspoilt setting.

We don't mind a lively nightlife, but appreciate some different and quieter alternatives too.
The Grand Strand has a great choice of theatres where you can catch a show and enjoy dinner – although it's not really what we Brits would call dinner – usually steak, salad and baked potato. There's the Carolina Opry and The Alabama

Theater offering variety shows.

My wife says we can't visit the USA and not shop.
Myrtle Beach has its share of great shopping malls selling every consumer product know to man.

We'd also like to see a little of the old Deep South while we're in South Carolina. Are there any places we can visit?
You get an instant feel of being in the Deep South at the golf clubs alone, as many have been created from former plantation land. Visit the Caledonia Golf and Fish Club – it's pure Gone With the Wind. You drive down a long alley lined with live oak trees, dripping with Spanish Moss and the clubhouse has a wide verandah with rocking chairs so you can unwind with a cooling drink as you gaze across the 18th hole. Just down the road is quaint, old fashioned Georgetown with its wide main street and its picturesque colour washed houses with old fashioned front porches and the Stars and Stripes flying from a flag pole in the garden. Charleston is about an hour's drive away but well worth the journey. It must be one of America's most picturesque towns.

Body &soul

Massages, aromatherapy, seaweed wraps, facials and golf. A varied mix of relaxation and sport to get your body and mind back in shape.

The LeSport complex is situated in a secluded bay on the northern tip of St Lucia.

Give us your body for a week and we'll give you back your mind." After a particularly stressful time at work, the invitation was too hard to dismiss. And when I found out that my body would be transported to St Lucia in the Caribbean for this transformation to take place I jumped at the chance. There was also the added attraction of championship-standard golf on the doorstep.

So off I jetted to The Body Holiday at LeSport in St Lucia on what proved to be the trip of a lifetime. Guests at LeSport can now play 18 holes of complimentary golf on the newly-designed course at the St Lucia Golf and Country Club. The fully-irrigated 6,829-yard par 71 championship course is just minutes from the resort, and transfers to and from the course are covered in the LeSport all-inclusive daily rate.

This is the only 18-hole course on St Lucia, set in the rolling hills of Cap Estate. It provides panoramic views of both the Atlantic and Caribbean and the island's tropical mountains. As well as having an idyllic setting this challenging course accommodates players of all levels from novice to professional. Club and shoe rentals and use of a cart are extra.

Designed by the American golf architect John Ponko, the course offers a variety of challenges with each hole having a character of its own, and where well-placed shots are rewarded and enjoyed by scratch and handicap golfers alike.

Originally, a 2,000-acre cotton and sugar cane farm, the plantation was developed as a golf course in 1968. More recently, the course has undergone a massive renovation and now lives up to

"The course offers a variety of challenges with each hole having a character of its own"

its championship status. And a holiday at LeSport gets you in the right frame of mind for playing your best golf.

LeSport is situated along one of St Lucia's most beautiful beaches and aims to offer its guests the ultimate in rest and relaxation – the complete 'body holiday'.

This exotic location is perfect for anyone needing to slowly unwind and allow their bodies to recuperate from the pressures of daily life. It offers the visitor the chance to enjoy a different pace of living. This is complemented by a range of restorative health treatments designed to rejuvenate both body and spirit.

At LeSport all guests can discover a different way of enjoying themselves, whether it be through deep rest and relaxation or trying a new sport or beauty treatment. Amid the colonnaded courtyards of the resort there are also saunas, plunge pools and an air-conditioned gym, and many other facilities for people to feel healthier and rejuvenated.

A wide range of land and watersports are available for the enthusiast and novice alike. Professional instruction is provided in all sports, including golf lessons before that challenging round on the championship course.

LeSport Factfile

The package: The vacation at LeSport is all-inclusive, combining the pleasures of a great active beach location with added benefits of sea water massage and beauty treatments.
Location: LeSport is situated on the north west tip of St Lucia. The resort sits directly on a secluded sandy beach and is surrounded by 18 acres of lush tropical gardens. It is 20 minutes from the capital Castries, and one-and-a-half hours from Hewanorra Airport.
The Hotel: There are 100 double bedrooms and two suites, many with four-poster beds. All accommodation is air-conditioned with private terraces. The bedrooms are exquisitely furnished and all have private bathrooms finished with Italian marble tiles.
Contact: Call for a free brochure on 0870 220 2344.
Website: www.lesport.com.lc

Le Sport

St Lucia Golf and Country Club

Castries

Hewanorra airport

Our 6 picks for
a Place in the Sun

Fed up with soggy fairways and temporary greens? Get away from those damp and cold winter days and find a place in the sun. Our six golfing hotspots will put the sharpness back into your game.

Words: **Steve Carr** Main photograph: **Bob Atkins**

South Africa's breathtaking beauty, gorgeous climate and laughable exchange rate make it the perfect golf destination. Erinvale is a course to savour.

SOUTH AFRICA:
The land of beauty

Why SOUTH AFRICA?

● Diverse, pulse-quickening and like smelling salts to your senses – the 'Rainbow Nation' is an incredible journey of discovery. Once apartheid was broken and the visitors came back to the land that tourists forgot, it soon became clear what a special place this is. News spreads fast and now cities like Cape Town and Durban, and the country's amazing game parks are showing their true colours.

For golf, the pleasant climate of the Cape and the Garden Route along to Port Elizabeth make them the favourites, but the established and new resort courses of Kwa Zulu Natal in the east are right behind. You can't also ignore the more 'African' north around Johannesburg.

There's the added benefits of an unbelievable exchange rate that means high living at incredibly low prices.

South Africa is a place of culture, infinite adventures under huge skies – from the bush to white-water rafting and wine tasting – and a land of wondrous beauty. Be prepared to be astounded.

Courses to savour

● Around the Cape try Erinvale, and Clovelly. Then Arabella at Hermanus and beyond, past the three astonishing courses at Fancourt to Sparresbosch at Knysna. To the east revel in Selbourne, Zimbali Lodge, Durban Country Club and Leopard's Creek. And if you want to enjoy all the fun of the fair and two breathtaking courses Sun City is for you.

Rain or Shine?

● Our winter is their summer. The Cape is the most temperate region but with average temperatures reaching 20°C in March and under an inch of rain, it shows how perfect the climate is for golf.

Nitty Gritty

● For the South African Tourist Board call 020 8944 8080 or visit www.satour.com. The currency is the rand.

Fancourt Golf Club. Tempted?

"You can be there for lunch and on the tee for an afternoon round without breaking sweat"

Vilamoura Old, one of seven Algarve courses ranked in Golf World's Top 100 of Continental European Courses.

2 | The Seasoned Choice

THE ALGARVE: The place for all-year-round sport

Why THE ALGARVE?

● As long-standing favourites go, this stretch of rocky bluffs, beaches and olive groves in southern Portugal is right up with the best. It offers golf for all tastes, a way of life that can be either understated and luxurious or raucous and lively. Fishing villages, where hauls of sardines are landed and then freshly laid onto the grills of the thousands of restaurants, mix with modern complexes and pastel villas that welcome the gently browning tourists. It is only just over two hours flying time from the UK, so not only can you take it easy for a week or more, but hop there for a short break when our winter is at its worst.

Golf is its main tourist industry despite the 'revolution' only beginning in 1965 at Penina. Now there are over 20 courses down the 150km strip, seven of them ranked in Golf World's Top 100 Courses of Continental Europe. The western end of the Algarve is quieter with fewer courses than the east which seems to have pockets of links that pop up every few miles.

But the golf must keep impressing because many people flock back year after year. Why? Because the golf and climate are known and dependable, and from leaving the UK you can be there for lunch and on the tee for an afternoon round without breaking sweat.

Courses to savour

● Where do you start? You could do no wrong with the seven in our Top 100, starting in the east and working west – San Lorenzo, Quinta do Lago, Val do Lobo (Royal), Vila Sol, Vilamoura Old, Vale da Pinta and Penina.

Rain or Shine?

● Because of its location golf is very much a year round hobby here – even in summer the Atlantic breezes can take the edge off the heat. But it is from October to April, when the golfing season is at its highest. It's never too warm with an average of 14°C, but days can easily climb into the low to mid 20s.

Nitty Gritty

● Call the Portugal Tourist Office in the UK on 09063 640640 or visit www.rtalgarve.pt or www.algarvegolfe.com.

Caledonia – one of the best courses out of more than 100 that stretch along the 60 miles of the Grand Strand.

3: | The Golfer's Choice

MYRTLE BEACH: Play, play, play

Why MYRTLE BEACH?

● For golf nuts, visiting this strip of South Carolina may feel like you've died and gone to heaven. It seems like around every corner there is a golf course beckoning you to test yourself on its manicured fairways. Over 100 courses, many of which are classy tests strewn with sand and water and cutting through pines and hopping over swamp, vie for your business on the 60-mile stretch known as the Grand Strand. And because of that green fees are extremely

competitive. You would be a fool indeed to come to this place and not golf, although if you didn't you can be royally entertained anyhow, on the miles of beach and at the many 'attractions'.

This may not be the most luxurious or best get-away-from-it-all destinations, but it is fun and sassy in its own homely style. Great for families as well as bands of hardened golfers who just want to play, play, play.

The courses too keep trying to outdo each other with a new approach or dare I say unique

way of attracting your attention, so you are never far away from cracking a smile. As far as value goes, it is as good as anywhere in the United States, and in world terms has as great a concentration of fine courses than anywhere, built by some of the most famed architects like Dye, Nicklaus and Trent Jones.

Courses to savour

● You could stick a pin in the list and you wouldn't go far wrong. But we'll plump for Arcadian Shores, Caledonia, Glen Dornach, Prestwick CC, True Blue, The Witch, Wild Wing and Wicked Stick – but don't hold us to that, ther are far too many good ones to call!

Rain or Shine?

● The average daily high is 19°C in March but that sneaks up into the mid 20s by April, which may help the beach dwellers among you too.

Nitty Gritty

● For more information call South Carolina Tourism in the UK on 01462 458028 or Coastal South Carolina on 001 843 805 3060

Kantaoui – the warmth comes from the desert but is cooled by sea breeze.

Southampton Princess – one of the best 18-hole, par-3 courses in the world.

4: The Discovery Choice

TUNISIA: Green fees at an affordable price

Why TUNISIA?
● Tunisia may be in Africa but it sits harmoniously on the Mediterranean Sea within shouting distance of Europe. And because it is a peaceful Moslem state, its influences are an intriguing mix of three continents, taking the best of each. It has a heartbeat that is Africa – vibrant and passionate. Its tolerant Arab roots are reflected in the customs and welcome, and Europe adds the modern edge. But all three are blended into its cuisine and architecture.

Golf is the country's fastest growing sport, even though there are still only eight courses. But they have pledged to build at least two more a year to attract the ever-growing band of golf lovers. Tunisia is fortunate to have over 1,200km of coastline, in the north backed by luxuriant forests, and to the south a moonscape of sandy dunes and palm groves, so loved by film makers. This mesmeric landscape which is punctuated by tourist towns is a haven for golf course architects to use the natural beauty, and the 'links' of Tabarka, Hammamet, Port El Kantaoui, Djerba and Monastir, offer incredible value for money, no little excitement and and all-year-round lushness and warmth to tantalise.

Courses to savour
● Tabarka in the north is cradled in a forest of eucalyptus and cork oaks, and together with both courses at Port El Kantaoui and the two in Hammamet – Golf Citrus and Yasmine – compete for the accolade of Tunisia's finest. You will not find an Augusta National, but instead good, honest courses, with green fees to smile about.

Rain or Shine?
● It has the luxury of benefiting from the warm desert climate but is cooled by the breezes off the sea. It can get very hot in summer with average temperatures in the high 20s, but in March the average is a respectable 14°C, meaning warm days and cool nights.

Nitty Gritty
● Tunisian National Tourist Board, tel 020 7224 5561; www.tourismtunisia.co.uk Currency is Dinars.

5: The Luxury Choice

BERMUDA: Good golf

Why BERMUDA?
● It may be just a dot in the ocean – just 25 miles long, a couple wide and 650 miles from the nearest landfall in North Carolina – but Bermuda is a rare pearl. Quaintly British but with an exotic and laid back edge all its own, rarely has anyone been and not be impressed by the friendliness of the people, the splendour of the landscape and the elegance of its the living. It is many people's idea of paradise.

Unique pink beaches nestle in rocky coves, smart and colourful houses and hotels cling to the hillsides of tropical vegetation, and the pace of life is calming and stress free. We have to be honest though. Because it is close to heaven on earth, it can not be for everyone. It has a reputation for coming at a price that not all can afford. That might be true, unless you weedle out the more local haunts where Bermudians will tell you that value can be found. It is amazing to think that eight courses have found room on this spit in the sea, but they have, and they will impress you with their quality. Despite the size of the island, golf does not dominate your eyeline or your senses – the way of life, abundant flora and fauna and restaurants to salivate at strike a brilliant balance.

Courses to savour
● Best known is Mid Ocean but very difficult to get on – but watch out for the all new Castle

for expensive tastes

Harbour, a major renovation set to thrill. Port Royal is enjoyable and boasts one of the most famous par-3s in the world perched on a cliffside. Bermuda also has one of the best par-3 courses in the world, all 18 holes of them at the Southampton Princess. Green fees are pricey.

Rain or Shine?
● Bermudians are spoiled. It may be a little breezy out there in the ocean but the average daily high never falls below 20°C even in winter. And the winter months are also its driest, although you are always looking out for the odd short, sharp shower.

Nitty Gritty
● Contact Bermuda Tourism on 020 7771 7001; www.bermudatourism.com.

Dubai Creek – one of Dubai's green oases amid the desert sand hills.

6: | The Mystical Choice

DUBAI: High-octane golfing experience

Why DUBAI?
● From one of the harshest landscapes for golf courses, up has sprung some laughably brilliant ones – oases of green among the sun-beaten desert sands. Feats of golfing engineering unsurpassed in the world, but with first class designs to back up their head-shaking existence. But while you are almost guaranteed cloudless skies and a sometimes searingly dry heat, Dubai is so much more. Transformed into a state of many riches thanks to the oilfields of the Arabian Peninsula, Dubai has immersed itself into the most modern of ways but still holds dear its traditional cultures.

Traders scurry around the souks of spice and gold beneath the most advanced buildings on earth, and the minorets still waft out their melodic chants while holidaymakers buzz around on jet-skis. Once a year the glitterati gather to watch the richest horse race on earth, the Dubai World Cup, yet still there are bedouin tribesmen herding goats and camels. There are few places on earth that can pack so much action into such a small area. Commerce, culture, sport and fun mingle together.

Courses to savour
● Only six 18-holers have been built, plus two nines, but all are unique experiences. How about playing the 'browns' of the Country Club, or driving under the floodlights of the Racing Club? Or you could just try the Emirates Club, Dubai Creek and the new Colin Montgomerie course at Emirates Hills. All three are vibrantly green and modern masters. In summer prices come down.

Rain or Shine?
● This is a desert, and so you can expect temperatures in the high 20s and 30s in the winter, going for ever upward in mid summer when they can soar to the high 40s. There is little humidity making the heat bearable, in fact it is a gorgeous warmth in winter, with almost zero rainfall. Perfect for a great golfing break.

Nitty Gritty
● Dubai Tourism www.dubaitourism.co.ae The currency is dirhams. The US dollar is also accepted.